Veseys Seeds
presents

SUMMER SAVOURY

Proven recipes from a season's harvest
of Vegetables and Berries

by

Faye Barrett
Eleanor MacDonald

COVER PHOTO

1. White Chocolate Fruit Tart, p.115
2. Poppy Seed Dressing, p.136
3. Three Green Salad, p.54
4. Asparagus Tart, p.8
5. Radish Cucumber Side Salad, p.87

Flower arrangement:

Lace flower, baby's breath in vase of brussels sprouts

Summer Savoury
Copyright © Vesey's Seeds Ltd.

1st Printing October, 2005; 2nd Printing February, 2006; 3rd Printing April, 2007; 4th Printing October, 2009; 5th Printing December, 2010; 6th Printing August, 2012

Library and Archives Canada Cataloguing in Publication

Barrett, Faye, 1950-
   Vesey's Seeds presents Summer Savoury : proven recipes from a season's harvest of vegetables and berries / by Faye Barrett, Eleanor MacDonald.

ISBN 0-9738907-0-3

   1. Cookery (Vegetables). 2. Cookery (Berries). I. MacDonald, Eleanor, 1953-   II. Veseys Seeds III. Title. IV. Title: Summer Savoury.

TX801.B295 2005   641.6'5
C2005-905018-7

Published by
Vesey's Seeds Ltd.
P.O.Box 9000
Charlottetown, PEI Canada C1A 8K6
telephone: 902-368-7333
facsimile: 902-368-3980
www.veseys.com

Photography: Louise Vessey
Design: John Barrett
Growing Tips: Angus Mellish
Props Assistance: Brenda MacDonald
Food Stylists: Faye Barrett, Eleanor MacDonald
Printing: Dollco Printing, Ottawa, Ontario, Canada

INTRODUCTION

Since 1939, Veseys Seeds have been delivering the promise of spring to gardeners throughout North America. Operating from our 40 acre research farm in the rural setting of York, Prince Edward Island, Veseys has grown to one of North America's leading mail order suppliers of vegetable and flower seeds, berries, roses, bulbs and perennials.

Throughout the decades Vesey's customers have welcomed the many and varied cookbooks scattered throughout the annual seed catalogue. In fact, one such cookbook reached 'Best Seller' status as a result of the many copies sold through Vesey's mailorder department.

For some time now we've thought that a *'Veseys'* authoritative Vegetable Cookbook was long overdue and so we finally began the production of *Summer Savoury*... the official Veseys Vegetable Cookbook!

We are pleased to showcase over 250 tested and proven recipes that not only feature the A to Zs of the vegetable family, but also some mouthwatering fruit dishes, dips, dressings, smoothies and stuffings. Everything contained in this comprehensive publication can be grown from the vast selection of seeds and plants offered each year by Veseys.

With the publication of *Summer Savoury*, it is our hope that gardening chefs of all ages will be further inspired to grow their own and deliver the freshest delights that nature has to offer. As always, we welcome your comments and sincerely hope that you enjoy this book as much as we've enjoyed taste-testing its contents.

Summer Savoury makes a great gift for friends and fellow gardeners at any time of year. Order yours today at www.veseys.com, call toll free 1-800-363-7333 or use the convenient order form found on page 161.

DEDICATION

Paderno Cookware

Table of Contents

Asparagus 8
Beans, Baking 10
Beans, Lima 12
Beans, Yellow/Green 12
Beets 16
Broccoli 22
Brussels Sprouts 25
Cabbage 27
Cantaloupe 31
Carrots 33
Cauliflower 40
Celery 42
Corn 43
Cucumber 46
Eggplant 48
Kale 51
Leeks 52
Lettuce 54
Okra 57
Onions 58
Parsnips 62
Peas 64
Peppers 67
Potatoes 69
Potatoes, Sweet 80
Pumpkin 84
Radish 87
Spinach 89
Squash 94
Swiss Chard 95
Tomatoes 96
Turnips 99
Watermelon 102
Zucchini 102
Blackberries 107
Blueberries 112
Kiwi 114
Raspberries 116
Rhubarb 118
Strawberries 120
Mixed Vegetable Dishes 124
Salad Dressings 133
Dips 138
Stuffings for Baked Potatoes 143
Glazes for Carrots 148
Drinks 149

*For a detailed listing by recipe, please refer
to the index starting on page 154*

Asparagus Tart

Flour	1 1/2 cups	375 ml
Salt	1/8 tsp	.5 ml
Garlic powder	1/2 tsp	2 ml
Dried mixed herbs	2 tsp	10 ml
Cold butter/margarine	5 tbsp	75 ml
Cold shortening	2 tbsp	30 ml
Cold water	3-5 tbsp	45-75 ml
Fresh asparagus	1 1/2 lbs	750 gm
Cream cheese	3 ounces	370 gm
Egg yolk	1	1
Blend cream	1 cup	250 ml
Whole eggs	3	3
Salt & Pepper	3/4 tsp	3 ml
Parmesan cheese	1/3 cup	75 ml
Chopped cooked ham	1 cup	250 ml

Combine first four ingredients, cut in butter and shortening until like pie crust. Sprinkle with water 1 tbsp at a time, stir till dough forms ball. On floured surface roll out to fit 10" tart pan. Freeze 10 min. Cut the asparagus into 2 1/2" pieces but save tips. Cut remaining pieces in half. Cook asparagus until crisp tender (4-5 min).

In bowl combine cream cheese and egg yolk, gradually add cream mixture (will be a little lumpy). Beat in eggs one at a time. Add salt and pepper (to taste). Place asparagus pieces (not tips) and ham over crust. Pour half the cream cheese mixture over top.

Bake @ 450° for 15 min. Pour remaining cream cheese mixture over top. Arrange tips on top, sprinkle with cheese. Bake at 350° for 40 min. Let stand 15 min. before cutting.

See photo front cover.

Almond Orange Asparagus

Fresh asparagus	2 lbs	1 kg
Butter or margarine	3/4 cup	175 ml
Orange juice	1/4 cup	50 ml
Grated orange peel	2 tsp	10 ml
Pepper	dash	dash
Seasoned salad almonds	1/2 cup	125 ml

In a saucepan bring 1 inch of water to a boil. Place asparagus in a steamer basket over water; cover and steam for 5 min. or until crisp-tender; drain. Place asparagus on a serving platter and keep warm.

In a skillet over medium heat, cook almonds in butter for 3-4 min until lightly browned. Add orange juice and peel; heat through.

Pour over asparagus, sprinkle with pepper.

Layered Asparagus

Whole wheat bread	12 slices	12 slices
Grated old cheddar	1 1/2 cups	375 ml
Fresh asparagus	1 - 1 1/2 lbs	500 - 750 gm
Diced cooked ham	2 cups	500 ml
Eggs	6	6
Milk	3 cups	750 ml
Dried minced onion	2 tbsp	30 ml
Salt	1/2 tsp	2 ml
Ground Mustard	1/4 tsp	1 ml

Using a doughnut cutter, cut 12 circles and holes from bread; set aside. Tear remaining bread in pieces and place in a greased 13" x 9" x 2" baking pan. Layer cheese, asparagus and ham over torn bread. Arrange bread circles and holes on top. Lightly beat eggs with milk. Add onion, salt and mustard; mix well. Pour egg mixture over bread circles and holes. Cover and refrigerate overnight. Bake uncovered at 325° for 55 minutes or until top is light golden brown. Let stand for ten minutes before serving.

See photo page 19.

Asparagus Rolls

Whole wheat bread	8 slices	8 slices
White bread	8 slices	8 slices
Cheese Whiz	16 tbsp	150 ml
Bacon	12 slices	12 slices
Asparagus	1 lb	500 g
Butter or margarine	as needed	as needed
Grated parmesan	as needed	as needed

Roll bread slices flat with a rolling pin. Spread each slice with about 2 teaspoons of Cheese Whiz. Sprinkle each slice with 3/4 tsp ground crisp bacon. Lay asparagus spear on end of each slice and trim any overhang. Roll up and secure with two toothpicks - one near each end of the roll. Brush each roll with melted butter; sprinkle with grated parmesan cheese. Arrange on an ungreased baking sheet. Bake at 400° F for 7 to 8 minutes until golden. Cut each roll in half and serve. Recipe makes 32 rolls. Do not freeze.

See photo page 38.

Hint! Stop picking asparagus once the shoots are smaller than a pencil. This will keep plant strong and healthy.

Asparagus Berry Salad

Fresh asparagus	1 lb	500 g
Olive oil	3 tbsp	45 ml
Salt	1/4 tsp	1 ml
Pepper	1/4 tsp	1 ml
Salad greens	8 cups	2000 ml
Strawberries	3 cups	750 ml
Red onion	1/3 onion sliced	1/3 onion sliced
Chopped pecans	1/2 cup	125 ml
Apple cider vinegar	2 tbsp	30 ml
Sugar	2 tsp	10 ml

In a bowl, toss 1 inch trimmed asparagus with 1 tablespoon oil. Spread in a single layer in a greased 15" x 10" x 1" baking pan. Sprinkle with salt and pepper. Bake at 400° for 15-20 minutes or until tender.

In a large salad bowl, toss greens, strawberries, onion, pecans and asparagus. In a small bowl whisk the vinegar, sugar and remaining 2 tablespoons of oil. Drizzle over salad and toss to coat. Serves 6-8.

Maple Baked Beans

Dried beans	2 - 2 1/2 cups	500 -625 ml
Chopped onions	2 med	2 med
Bacon chopped	1 lb	125 ml
Molasses	1/2 cup	15 ml
Sugar	1 tbsp	10 ml
Vinegar	2 tsp	10 ml
Salt	2 tsp	60 ml
Ketchup	1/4 cup	15 ml
Mustard	1 tbsp	125 ml
Maple syrup	1/2 cup	

Cover beans with water and soak overnight. Next day remove any discoloured beans. Use the soaking water and bring the beans and water to a boil (additional water may be needed to cover the beans). Simmer slowly for approx. 30 minutes or until tender.

Combine the remaining ingredients with the beans in a greased casserole. Bake covered at 250° for 5 hours, then 325° for 2 hours.

Saturday Night Baked Beans

Dried beans	1 1/2-2 cups	375 - 500 ml
Small onion	1	1
Molasses	1/4 cup	60 ml
Ketchup	1/4 cup	60 ml
Prepared mustard	1 tbsp	15 ml
Salt	1 tsp	5 ml
Pepper	1/2 tsp	2 ml
White vinegar	2 tbsp	30 ml
Worcestershire sauce	1 tsp	5 ml
Bacon - cut in pieces	4-5 strips	4-5 strips
Boiling water	1/2 cup	125 ml
Crushed pineapple	1/2 cup	125 ml

Cover beans with water and soak overnight. Next day remove any discoloured beans. Use the soaking water and bring the beans and water to a boil (additional water may be needed to cover the beans). Simmer slowly for approx. 30 minutes or until tender.

In a greased bean pot or casserole, put chopped onion on bottom. Mix all other ingredients (except boiling water, bacon and pineapple), and pour this sauce on top of the onion. Place beans on top of sauce and then pour boiling water on top to just barely cover beans. Top this mixture with the bacon pieces.

Bake covered in a 250° oven for about 7 hours. After 4 hours, remove from oven and mash some of the beans. Stir and return covered pot to the oven. After 6 hours, remove the cover until done; add crushed pineapple to the mixture during this final hour. If needed, add water and stir.

See photo page 55.

Rush Hour Beans

Baked beans	2 lg cans	2 lg cans
Ground beef	1/2 lb	250 g
Small onion	1	1
Butter	2 tbsp	30 ml
Ketchup	1/2 cup	125 ml
Brown sugar	3 tbsp	45 ml
Applesauce	3/4 cup	175 ml
Worcestershire sauce	1 tbsp	15 ml
Salt	to taste	to taste

Brown beef and onion in butter. Combine remaining ingredients. Place in large casserole. Bake at 325° for 45 minutes.

Barbecued Lima Beans

Dried lima beans	1 lb	500 g
Water	6 cups	1500 ml
Chopped onion	1 cup	250 ml
Salt	1 tsp	5 ml
Ketchup	1 cup	250 ml
Brown sugar	3/4 cup	175 ml
Maple pancake syrup	1/3 cup	75 ml
Hot pepper sauce	1/4 tsp	1 ml
Crumbled bacon	4 strips	4 strips

Place beans in a saucepan, add water to cover by 2 inches. Bring to a boil; boil for 2 minutes. Remove from heat, cover, let stand for 1 hour. Drain and rinse; discard water.

Return beans to saucepan, add 6 cups of water, onions and salt. Bring to a boil. Reduce heat, cover and simmer for 1 3/4 hours or until tender. Drain.

Stir in ketchup, brown sugar, syrup, hot pepper sauce and bacon. Transfer to casserole. Cover and bake at 350° for 30 minutes. Uncover and bake an additional 30 minutes

Three Colour Bean Salad

Green beans	1 1/2 cups	375 ml
Yellow beans	1 1/2 cups	375 ml
Red kidney beans	1 cup	250 ml
Green pepper	half	half
Chopped onion	2 tbsp	30 ml
White sugar	3/4 cup	175 ml
White vinegar	2/3 cup	150 ml
Salad oil	1/3 cup	75 ml
Salt	1 tsp	5 ml
Pepper	1 tsp	5 ml

Cook all beans until tender but not mushy; place beans in a covered jar. Separately, mix together all other ingredients after finely chopping the green pepper. Pour mixture over beans and let marinate over night in the refrigerator. Keeps well.

Hint! If squeezing fresh orange, lemon or lime juice, save the rinds in zip lock bags and freeze until needed. They freeze well!

Dill Beans

White vinegar	1 cup	250 ml
Water	1/2 cup	125 ml
Garlic clove	1	1
Dill	1 head	1 head
Pickling salt	1 tsp	5 ml
Yellow beans	2 cups	500ml

Bring the vinegar and water to a boil in a nonreactive saucepan to form a brine. Separately pack each clean preserving jar with the garlic, one sprig of dill and salt. Pack in the yellow beans leaving 1/2 inch headspace. Pour the hot brine over the beans again leaving a 1/2 inch headspace.

Process in a boiling water bath for 10 minutes. Cool undisturbed for 12 hours. Store in a cool dry place. Do not open jars for six weeks to allow the flavours to develop.

This recipe is designed to be multiplied or used with green beans. You may omit the canning step and leave in the refrigerator.

Simple Summer Beans

Yellow beans	1 lb	500 g
Green beans	1 lb	500 g
Finely chopped onion	2 tbsp	30 ml
Olive oil	2 tbsp	30 ml
Vinegar	1 tbsp	15 ml
Minced garlic	1 clove	1 clove
Salt	1/2 tsp	2 ml
Pepper	1/4 tsp	1 ml
TOPPING:		
Dry bread crumbs	2 tbsp	30 ml
Grated parmesan	2 tbsp	30 ml
Melted butter	1 tbsp	15 ml

In a saucepan, cover beans with water. Cook until crisp-tender; drain. Add onion, oil, vinegar, garlic, salt and pepper; toss to coat. Transfer to an ungreased 2 qt baking dish. Toss crumbs, cheese and butter; sprinkle over bean mixture.

Bake uncovered at 350° for 20-25 minutes or until golden brown. Makes 6-8 servings.

Hint!   Dark seeded beans are much more tolerent of cold spring soil than white seeded beans.

13

Green Beans with Onions

Green beans	2 lbs	1 kg
Onions	4 large	4 large
Olive oil	1/4 cup	60 ml
Salt	to taste	to taste
Pepper	to taste	to taste

Prepare beans by cutting into 3 or 4 pieces each. Cut the onions in half and slice very thin.

In a large frying pan, heat the oil over medium heat. When it's hot add the onions. Sauté for a few minutes until the onions become translucent. Reduce to low heat and cook until the onions turn a rich caramel colour (20-25 minutes).

Rinse beans; drain. Add beans to the onions, stir and cook for about 40 minutes, stirring occasionally. These beans should be limp when ready to serve. Season with salt and pepper. Serve hot or at room temperature.

Beans and Veggie Primavera

Yellow beans	1/4 lb	125 g
Green beans	1/4 lb	125 g
Chopped red pepper	1/2	.5
Carrot (thinly sliced)	1	1
Olive oil	1-2 tbsp	15-30 ml
Minced garlic	1 clove	1 clove
Chicken stock	1/4 cup	60 ml
Tomato sauce	14 oz can	375 g
Basil	1 tsp	5 ml
Oregano	1 tsp	5 ml
Chopped green onions	2	2
Pasta	14 oz can	375 g
Grated parmesan	1/4 cup	60 ml

Trim beans into 1 inch lengths. Heat oil, cook beans and garlic while stirring - 2 minutes.

Add other prepared vegetables, cook until softened. Pour in stock and steam until all are tender crisp. Add tomato sauce and seasonings. Cook until heated. Add salt and pepper to taste.

Cook your favourite pasta, drain and toss with vegetables. Sprinkle with parmesan.

Herb, Pine Nut Green Beans

Green beans	1 1/2 lbs	750 g
Pine nuts	2 tbsp	30 ml
Dill or parsley	1/4 cup	60 ml
Butter or margarine	1 tbsp	15 ml
Lemon juice	2 tsp	10 ml
Salt	to taste	to taste
Pepper	to taste	to taste

Toast nuts in 350° oven for 5 minutes until golden. In a large saucepan of boiling water, cook beans for 5 minutes or until tender-crisp. Drain thoroughly. Add dill (parsley) and melted butter, toss gently. Add lemon juice, add salt and pepper to taste. Sprinkle with pine nuts. Makes 10 servings

Summer Green Bean Salad

Yellow beans	1 cup	250 ml
Green beans	1 cup	250 ml
Sliced celery	1/2 cup	125 ml
Sliced cucumber	1/2 cup	125 ml
Sliced radish	4	4
Tomato (wedges)	4 medium	4 medium
Lettuce (your choice)	1 head	1 head

After cooking and draining the beans together, toss in bowl along with lettuce and other vegetables. A great dressing for this salad is the Golden Green Bean Salad Dressing found on page 135.

"This is the kind of cookbook I love best because every page shows so much care and attention. Hats off to Faye and Eleanor for creating and presenting everything in such a mouth-watering way."
Aldona Satterthwaite, Editor, Canadian Gardening

15

Beet Relish

Cooked beets	5 cups	1250 ml
White vinegar	3 cups	750 ml
White sugar	2 cups	500 ml
Turmeric	1 tsp	5 ml
Dry mustard	1 tsp	5 ml
White flour	1/2 cup	125 ml

Cook beets as usual. Remove skins and dice finely. Heat the white sugar with 2 1/2 cups of vinegar. Mix the other 1/2 cup of vinegar with the dry ingredients, then add to the heated sugar mixture on stove.

Please note: *Add a little of the hot sugar/vinegar mixture to the dry ingredients mixture, before adding all of the dry ingredient mixture to the hot mixture. For those new to preserving, this will avoid your mixture going lumpy as this step will help heat up your dry ingredients.*

Continue heating and whisking until ingredients are completely mixed and cooked. Add diced beets and heat through. Bottle in sterilized mason jars.

See photo page 74.

Beets Russian

Cooked, cubed beets	2 cups	500 ml
French dressing	1/2 cup	125 ml
Minced green onion	1/2 cup	125 ml
Whipped sour cream	1 cup	250 ml

Fold all ingredients together in saucepan and heat gently or place all in a baking dish and bake 350° for 20-25 minutes.

See photo page 92.

Hint! After peeling and cooking beets, use an egg slicer. Perfect slices every time.

Tasty Baked Beets

Shredded, peeled beets	4 cups	1000 ml
Shredded onion	1 med	1 med
Shredded potato	1 med	1 med
Brown sugar	3 tbsp	45 ml
Vegetable oil	3 tbsp	45 ml
Water	2 tbsp	30 ml
Vinegar	1 tbsp	15 ml
Salt	1/2 tsp	2 ml
Pepper	1/4 tsp	1 ml
Ginger	1/4 tsp	1 ml
Ground cloves	1/4 tsp	1 ml
Cinnamon	1/4 tsp	1 ml

In a large bowl, combine beets, onion and potato; set aside. In a small bowl, combine brown sugar, oil, water, vinegar and seasonings. Pour over vegetables; toss to coat.

Pour into a greased 1 1/2 quart baking dish. Cover and bake at 350° for 45 minutes, stirring occasionally. Uncover and bake 15-25 minutes longer until vegetables are tender. Makes 8 to 10 servings.

Better Pickled Beets

Beets	2 lbs	1 kg
Red wine vinegar	1 1/2 cups	375 ml
Honey	3/4 cup	175 ml
Dry mustard	2 tbsp	30 ml
Salt	1/2 tsp	2 ml
Onion, diced	1 med	1 med

Cook beets and save 1 cup of beet liquid. Peel off skins and slice. Bring other ingredients to a boil in a separate pot. Put beets in jars, mix beet liquid with cooked mixture. Pour over beets and seal. Store in a dry, cool place.

17

Beet and Potato Mash

Beets	1 1/3 lbs	650 g
Potatoes	1 1/4 lbs	600 g
Cream	2 tbsp	30 ml
Sugar	1/2 tsp	2 ml
Butter	2 oz	50 g

Boil, steam or microwave beets and potatoes separately until tender (see below). Drain and peel while warm. Coarsley chop beets and potatoes; blend or process with remaining ingredients until pureed. Best made just before serving. Can be served cold on a bed of lettuce.

COOKING BEETS: based on 3 medium beets (500 g)

BOIL: add beets to medium pan of boiling water; boil uncovered about 45 minutes or until tender. Drain, peel while still warm.

STEAM: place beets in steamer basket; cook, covered, over pan of simmering water about 55 minutes or until tender. Drain, peel while still warm.

MICROWAVE: place beets and 2 tbsp water in large microwave-safe dish. Cover, microwave on high about 30 minutes or until tender, pausing halfway through to turn. Drain, peel while still warm.

Ladies' Lunch

1. Canteloupe Fruit Toss, page 31
2. Sweet Potato Scones, page 83
3. Tomato Cheese Pie, page 98
4. Scrumptious Broccoli Salad, page 23
5. Layered Asparagus, page 9

Flower arrangement:

Dianthus 'Telstar Mix', Aster 'Ballet Mix', Aster 'Oster Feather Crimson', Cosmos Sensation Mix.

Harvard Beets

Diced, cooked beets	1 lb	500 g
White sugar	2 tbsp	30 ml
Cornstarch	1 tbsp	15 ml
Salt	1/4 tsp	1 ml
White vinegar	1/4 cup	60 ml
Butter	2 tbsp	30 ml
Water	1/3 cup	75 ml

Combine sugar, cornstarch and salt. Stir in water, vinegar and butter. Cook in a double boiler until mixture thickens. Add beets and heat. Serve hot!

Orange Marinade for Beets

Oil	3/4 cup	175 ml
Red wine vinegar	1/3 cup	75 ml
Orange juice	3 tbsp	45 ml
Lemon juice	1 tbsp	15 ml
Nutmeg	1/4 tsp	1 ml
Cinnamon	1/4 tsp	1 ml

Combine ingredients, pour over cooked beets. Refrigerate overnight.

Just Desserts

1. Cinnamon Choc. Fruit Tart, page 111
2. Upside Down S.Potato Cake, page 84
3. Sweet Potato Layer Cake, page 80

Flowers:

Hydrangea 'Nikko Blue'.

Broccoli and Corn Bake

Broccoli	2 cups	500 ml
Cream style corn	16 oz can	500 g
Crushed Ritz crackers	1/2 cup	125 ml
Egg (beaten)	1	1
Onion	1 tbsp	15 ml
Pepper	dash	dash

Cook and chop the broccoli. In a bowl, combine the corn, broccoli, half the quantity of crushed crackers, egg, onion and pepper. Place in a greased 1 - 1 1/2 quart baking dish. Sprinkle with remaining Ritz crackers. Cover and bake at 350° for 45 minutes. Serves 6.

See photo page 128.

Broccoli Vegetable Pie

Butter	1/2 cup	125 ml
Whole wheat flour	1 1/4 cups	300 ml
Baking powder	2 tsp	10 ml
Salt	1/2 tsp	2 ml
Plain yogurt	1/2 cup	125 ml

Filling:		
Fine chopped broccoli	2 cups	500 ml
Diced onion	1/3 cup	75 ml
Grated cheese	1 cup	250 ml
Sliced tomatoes	2 medium	2 medium
Mayonnaise	1/3 cup	75 ml
Basil	1 tsp	5 ml
Garlic powder	1/2 tsp	2 ml

Cut butter into flour, baking powder & salt. Add yogurt to crumb mixture. Put the dough into greased 9 or 10 inch pan. Layer filling over crust in order given ending with mayonnaise and seasonings.
Bake at 450° for 10 minutes, then at 350° for 30 minutes.

Broccoli and Cauliflower Bake

Cauliflower	1 med. head	1 med. head
Broccoli	1 lb	500 g
Butter	1 1/2 tbsp	22 ml
Flour	2 tbsp	30 ml
Salt	1 tsp	5 ml
Nutmeg	1/4 tsp	1 ml
Tarragon leaves	1 tsp	5 ml
Lemon juice	1 tbsp	15 ml
Milk	1 cup	250 ml
Cream cheese	1 pkg	125 g
Butter	2 tbsp	30 ml
Bread crumbs	1/3 cup	75 ml
Grated cheese	3/4 cup	175 ml
Chopped parsley	sprinkle	sprinkle

Break cauliflower and broccoli into florets and cook until tender crisp (add some lemon juice to water to keep cauliflower nice and white). Drain well and arrange attractively in a 3 quart casserole dish. In saucepan, melt butter. Blend in flour, seasonings, lemon juice and milk. Cook until thickened. Blend in cream cheese. Stir until smooth. Pour sauce over vegetables. Toss melted butter and bread crumbs. Sprinkle evenly over sauce. Top with grated cheese. Bake at 350° until heated through and cheese is melted (20-30 minutes). Garnish with finely chopped parsley.

See photo page 92.

Scrumptious Broccoli Salad

Chopped broccoli	1 head	1 head
Chopped green onions	2 stalks	2 stalks
Grated carrots	2	2
Chopped celery	3 stalks	3 stalks
Raisins	1/2 - 3/4 cup	125-175 ml
Sugar	1/8 - 1/4 cup	30-60 ml
Miracle Whip	1 cup	250 ml
Vinegar	2 tbsp	30 ml

Combine broccoli, green onions, carrots, celery and raisins. Mix sugar, Miracle Whip and vinegar together, then mix with salad ingredients.

See photo page 19.

23

Broccoli Slaw Salad

Shredded broccoli stems	4 cups	1000 ml
Carrot	1/2	.5
Shredded purple cabbage	1/8 cup	30 ml
Sunflower seeds	3/4 cup	175 ml
Green onions	1/4 cup	60 ml
Toasted almonds	1/2 cup	125 ml
Dried beef soup noodles	1 pkg	1 pkg

Break up noodles and mix with the shredded vegetables, onion, almonds and seeds.

DRESSING

Olive oil	1/2 cup	125 ml
White vinegar	1/3 cup	75 ml
Granulated sugar	1/2 cup	125 ml

In a saucepan, heat above ingredients until sugar is dissolved. Add flavour packet from Noodles package. Stir until dissolved. Cool. Pour over salad ingredients and mix well. Cover and refrigerate.

Cheesy Broccoli Pie

Cooked broccoli	2 cups	500 ml
Sliced mushrooms	1 cup	250 ml
Chopped onion	3/4 cup	175 ml
Butter	2 tbsp	30 ml
Grated cheddar	1 cup	250 ml
Tea biscuit mix	1/2 cup	125 ml
Salt	1/2 tsp	2 ml
Pepper	1/8 tsp	.5 ml
Eggs	3	3
Milk	1 cup	250 ml

Melt butter in frying pan. Add onions and mushrooms. Sauté until soft. Grease 9" pie plate. Spread onion/mushroom mixture on bottom of pan. Sprinkle with broccoli and then cheese.

Mix or blend milk, eggs, biscuit mix, salt and pepper. Pour on top of cheese. Bake in a 400° oven for 25-35 minutes. Test for doneness with a knife. Cuts into six to eight pieces.

See photo page 145.

Delicious Brussels Sprouts

Brussels sprouts	2 lb	1 kg
Butter	3 tbsp	45 ml
Flour	3 tbsp	45 ml
Milk	2 cups	500 ml
Dijon mustard	1 tsp	5 ml
Salt	3/4 tsp	3.5 ml
Pepper	1/2 tsp	2 ml
Nutmeg	1/4 tsp	1 ml
Cheddar cheese	1 cup	250 ml

Cut an X in the base of each sprout. Cook in a large saucepan of boiling water for 7-9 minutes (better tender-crisp than overdone). Drain and refresh under cold water (gives that nice green colour). Press out excess cold water with towel. Cool. Halve and set aside.

In a saucepan melt butter over medium heat. Stir in flour and cook, stirring for 3-5 minutes or until smooth and thickened. Stir in mustard, salt, pepper, nutmeg and milk. Remove from heat. Stir in half of the cheese (shredded) until melted. Gently stir in brussels sprouts. Spoon into greased 11 x 7 inch baking dish. Sprinkle with remaining shredded cheese. Bake at 350° for approximately 30 minutes or until bubbly. Brown under broiler for 2 minutes.

Lemon Glazed Brussels Sprouts

Brussels sprouts	1 lb	500 g
Melted butter	2 tbsp	30 ml
Lemon juice	2 tbsp	30 ml
Grated lemon peel	2 tsp	10 ml
Salt	1/4 tsp	1 ml
Lemon-pepper seasoning	1/4 tsp	1 ml
Toasted sliced almonds	1/4 cup	60 ml

Cook brussels sprouts until tender and drain. Stir in the butter, lemon juice, lemon peel, salt and lemon pepper. Sprinkle with almonds. Serves 4 and is a delicious alternative for those who think they don't like brussels sprouts!

Hint! Pinch the top off Brussels Sprouts in early September to encourage the sprouts to form.

Brussels Sprouts Casserole

Brussels sprouts	2 lbs	1 kg
Water chestnuts	1 can	1 can
Mushrooms	1 can	1 can
Sour cream	8 oz	250 g
Cream mushroom soup	1 can	1 can
Onion soup mix	1 pkg	1 pkg
Rice Krispies	1 cup	250 ml
Melted butter	3 tbsp	45 ml

Cook brussels sprouts until tender - don't overcook. Add drained water chestnuts, drained mushrooms, sour cream and both soups. Put in large casserole. Top with Rice Krispies tossed in butter. Bake at 350° for 45 minutes.

Brown Sugar Glazed Sprouts

Brussels sprouts	2 cups	500 ml
Butter	1 tbsp	15 ml
Brown sugar	2 tsp	10 ml
Chopped pecans	2 tbsp	30 ml
Salt	to taste	to taste
Pepper	to taste	to taste

Trim base of sprouts and outside leaves. Steam sprouts over boiling water for about 10 minutes or until tender. Drain thoroughly.

In skillet, melt butter over medium heat; add sugar and stir until melted. Add sprouts and pecans; stir to coat well and cook for 1 to 2 minutes. Season with salt and pepper to taste. Serves 4.

See photo page 127.

Stuffed Cabbage Rolls

Large green cabbage	1	1

FOR THE MEAT:

Ground beef	2 lbs	1 kg
Converted rice	1/2 cup	125 ml
Sautéed onions	1/2 cup	125 ml
Eggs	2	2
Crushed garlic	1/2 tbsp	7.5 ml
Salt	1 tsp	5 ml
Pepper	1/2 tsp	2 ml

FOR THE POT:

Diced onions	3 med	3 med
Diced tomatoes	4 cups	1000 ml
Tomato sauce	8 oz can	250 g can
Lemon juice	3 tbsp	45 ml
Wine (sweet or dry)	1/4 cup	60 ml
Brown sugar	2 tbsp	30 ml
Ginger snaps	8	8
Water	1/2 cup	125 ml
Salt	1 1/2 tsp	7 ml
Raisins	1/2 cup	125 ml

Cut off slice from bottom of cabbage; cut as much core as possible. Wash cabbage well. Boil a large pot full of water. Immerse cabbage in water and allow it to boil for a few minutes. As soon as leaves start to wilt slightly, take cabbage out, drain and remove outer leaves or as many as have wilted. This may take some repeating until you have been able to remove most of the leaves easily - be careful not to tear leaves.

Drain leaves on paper towel. Blend all the items for the meat in one bowl. On each cabbage leaf place 1 tbsp of meat on the end closest to you. Bring cabbage end over meat. Fold both vertical sides over towards centre and roll up the package. Continue until all the meat is used.

Use a 5 or 6 quart Dutch oven or oven casserole. Line the bottom with dried onion and cabbage shreds (leftover cabbage not used for rolls).

Place cabbage rolls in neat layers. Cover with all the remaining ingredients. Cook for 2 hours over low heat tightly covered. They may also be baked in the oven at 350° for 2 hours. Serves 6.

Hint! When cooking cabbage, add a bit of vinegar to the pan to keep it from losing its colour.

Honey Mustard Slaw

Shredded cabbage	3 cups	750 ml
Shredded carrots	2 med	2 med
Chopped apple	1 cup	250 ml
Salad oil	3 tbsp	45 ml
Dijon mustard	3 tbsp	45 ml
Lemon juice	2 tbsp	30 ml
Honey	2 tbsp	30 ml
Clove garlic	1	1
Chopped cashews	2 tbsp	30 ml

In a large bowl stir together cabbage, carrots and the coarsley chopped apple (pear makes an interesting substitute for apple). Set aside.

For dressing, in a mason jar, combine oil, mustard, lemon juice, honey and garlic. Cover and shake well; pour over cabbage mixture. Toss to coat, cover and chill for at least 2 hours.

Sprinkle with nuts just prior to serving. Makes 4 to 6 servings.

Cheddar Cabbage Casserole

Crushed Honey Nut Cornflakes	2 1/2 cups	625 ml
Melted butter	1/2 cup	250 ml
Shredded cabbage	4 1/2 cups	1125 ml
Chopped onion	1/4 cup	60 ml
Salt	1/4 tsp	1 ml
Pepper	1/4 tsp	1 ml
Condensed cream of mushroom soup	10 3/4 oz can	325 g
Milk	1 cup	250 ml
Mayonnaise	1/2 cup	125 ml
Shredded old cheddar cheese	2 cups	500ml

Toss the cornflakes and butter; sprinkle half into a greased 13 x 9 x 2 inch baking dish. Layer with the cabbage, onion, salt and pepper. In a bowl, combine the soup, milk and mayonaise until smooth. Spoon over top; sprinkle with cheese and remaining cornflake mixture. Bake, uncovered, at 350° for 45-50 minutes or until golden brown. Makes 8-10 servings.

Red Cabbage with Apples

Chopped onion	1 medium	1 medium
Butter	1/4 cup	60 ml
Shredded red cabbage	2 lbs	1 kg
Salt	1/2 tsp	2 ml
Pepper	1/4 tsp	1 ml
Brown sugar	1/4 cup	60 ml
Apple cider	1 cup	250 ml
White wine vinegar	2 tbsp	30 ml
Gravenstein apples	2	2
Fresh parsley	1 tbsp	15 ml

In a large skillet, sauté onion in butter until tender but not brown. Add the cabbage, salt, pepper, brown sugar, cider, vinegar and apples (peeled and chopped). Cover and simmer until the cabbage and apples are tender and the liquid is reduced - about 1 hour. Sprinkle with fresh parsley and serve. Makes 6 to 8 servings.

Cabbage and Apple Treat

Red cabbage	1 medium	1 medium
Cooking apple	1 med	1 med
Water	1/3 cup	75 ml
Red wine vinegar	1/4 cup	60 ml
Salt	to taste	to taste
Pepper	to taste	to taste
Honey	2 tbsp	30 ml

Slice cabbage. Peel, core and slice apple. In large skillet or heavy pan, combine cabbage, apple, water and vinegar. Stir and bring to a boil. Reduce heat and simmer, covered, stirring occasionally, for 1 hour or until cabbage is very tender.

Stir in salt, pepper and honey to taste. Makes 4 servings.

Surprise Coleslaw

Vanilla Ice Cream	1/2 cup	125 ml
Mayonnaise	1/4 cup	60 ml
Prepared mustard	1 tsp	5 ml
Salt	1/4 tsp	1 ml
Pepper	dash	dash
Green cabbage	2 cups	500 ml
Red cabbage	1 cup	250 ml
Shredded carrot	1 medium	1 medium

In a large bowl, combine ice cream, mayonnaise, mustard, salt and pepper until smooth. Add cabbage and carrot; mix well. Cover and chill for at least 1 hour. Serves 4.

See photo page 74.

Cabbage Tomato Stir Fry

Shredded cabbage	4 cups	1000 ml
Diced tomatoes	2 cups	500 ml
Chopped onions	1 med	1 med
Green pepper	1 med	1 med
Yellow pepper	1 med	1 med
Margarine	2 tbsp	30 ml
Salt	1/2 tsp	2 ml
Parsley	1 tsp	5 ml
Tarragon	1 tsp	5 ml

In a non stick skillet, sauté the cabbage, tomatoes, onion and green pepper in margarine until vegetables are tender, about 20 minutes. Season with salt, parsley and tarragon. Serves 6.

Cantaloupe Fruit Toss

Large cantaloupe	1	1
Large pineapple	1/2	.5
Kiwi	3	3
Maraschino cherries	1/2 cup	125 ml
Sour cream	1/3 cup	75 ml
Honey	1 tbsp	15 ml
Shredded coconut	1/4 cup	60 ml

Peel, core and cut pineapple into 1" chunks. Cut melon into quarters and scoop into balls leaving a little flesh on the rind.

In a large bowl, combine pineapple and cantaloupe balls, peeled and diced kiwi and halved cherries. Divide fruit evenly among the 4 quarters of the cantaloupe rinds. In a separate bowl, combine sour cream and honey; top fruit with mixture. Sprinkle with coconut. Garnish with mint sprigs if so desired.

See photo page 19.

Cantaloupe Special

Cantaloupe	1 large	1 large
Orange juice	3 tbsp	45 ml
Maple syrup	3 tbsp	45 ml
Red seedless grapes	1 cup	250 ml
Kiwi	3	3
Leaf lettuce	1 head	1 head
Pineapple, cut in chunks	1 cup	250 ml
Shredded coconut	1/4 cup	60 ml

Cut 6 rings, about 1/2 inch wide from the center section of the cantaloupe. Remove seeds and set rings aside. Cube the remaining cantaloupe.

In a bowl, combine orange juice and maple syrup. Add grapes, kiwi (peeled, quartered and sliced), and cubed cantaloupe and pineapple; stir gently to coat. Place cantaloupe rings on lettuce; top with fruit and sprinkle with coconut.

Serves six.

Hint! Use a wooden spoon when seeding melons like cantaloupe or honeydew. You are less likely to gouge the flesh.

Cantaloupe Fruit Cup

Cantaloupe cubed	2 cups	500 ml
Kiwi sliced	2	2
Green grapes halved	1 cup	250 ml
Strawberries halved	1 cup	250 ml
Blueberries	1 cup	250 ml
Sour cream	1/2 cup	125 ml
Honey	1 tbsp	15 ml
Orange juice	1 tbsp	115 ml

In a large bowl combine kiwi, cantaloupe, grapes, strawberries and blueberries. In a small bowl, combine sour cream, honey and orange juice; pour over fruit and toss to coat. Serve immediately. Makes 8-10 servings.

Show-off Melon Treat

Strawberry jello	3 oz pkg	85 g pkg
Boiling water	1 cup	250 ml
Cold water	3/4 cup	175 ml
Cantaloupe	1 medium	1 medium

Dissolve jello powder in boiling water in a medium bowl. Stir until no granules are visible. Stir in cold water. Chill until it is as thick as unbeaten egg whites - about 1 1/2 hours.

While jello chills, prepare the cantaloupe. Cut melon in half crosswise and remove the seeds. Using the the small end of a melon-ball cutter, remove balls around the outer edge of the melon and from the center, leaving a 1/4 inch shell (be very careful to not cut through the skin). Invert shells on paper towel. Put 1 cup of the melons balls aside, save rest for snacks.

When jello has reached thickness as above, stir in the melon balls. Place each cantalope half in a dish large enough to support it and keep it level. Spoon jello into the melon cavities. If all the mixture doesn't fit, pour into a small dish and refrigerate separately. Chill melon molds until firm; about 3 hours.

Remove cantaloupe from dishes. Cut each in half to make wedges. Garnish your plate with mint leaves for extra effect. Serves 4 people who will all think you're a melon magician.

See photo page 110.

Hint! Do not start melons more than 4-5 weeks before putting them out. If the plants are too large, they will be set back.

Cream of Carrot Soup

Sliced Carrots	3 cups	750 ml
Yellow onion	1 large	1 large
Butter	1/2 cup	125 ml
Sugar	1 tsp	5 ml
Salt	1 tsp	5 ml
Pepper	1 tsp	5 ml
Diced potato	1 medium	1 medium
Water	1/2 cup	125 ml
Light cream	1 1/2 cups	375 ml
Flour	4 tbsp	60 ml
Milk	4 1/2 cups	1000 ml
Paprika	dash	dash
Cayenne pepper	dash	dash
Minced garlic	1 clove	1 clove
Croutons	1/2 cup	125 ml

Sauté carrots and chopped onion in large pot in 4 tbsp of butter for a few minutes. Add sugar, salt, potato and water. Cover and simmer until vegetables are tender. Purée vegetables in a blender with cream.

Melt rest of butter in a skillet and stir in flour to form a roux and cook until golden. Heat the milk and stir into roux with a whisk. Cook white sauce until thickened.

Combine carrot purée and white sauce in a large pot. Add some pepper, paprika and cayenne to taste as well as a little minced garlic and salt. Simmer the soup gently for another 10-15 minutes, stirring occasionally. Serve hot, garnished with croutons. Serves 8.

See photo page 55.

Carrot Country Pie

Grated carrots	4 cups	1000 ml
Crushed Ritz crackers	2 cups	500 ml
Grated cheddar cheese	1 1/2 cups	375 ml
Chopped onion	1/2 cup	125 ml
Butter	1/2 cup	125 ml

In a bowl, mix carrots, crackers, 1/2 cup cheese, onion and butter. Reserve 1 cup cheese for topping. Add a dash of salt and pepper. Place in a pie plate. Cut several Ritz crackers in half and stand them up around the edge of the pie plate. Top with cheese and bake at 350° for 30-45 minutes.

Hint! The flavour of carrots and parsnips improves after the first couple of frosts.

33

Sweet and Sour Carrots

Sliced carrots	3 cups	750 ml
Chopped onion	1	1
Chopped green pepper	1	1
Tomato soup	1 can	1 can
Sugar	1 cup	250 ml
Salad oil	1/2 cup	125 ml
White vinegar	3/4 cup	175 ml
Salt	1 tsp	5 ml

Cook sliced carrots separately until tender crisp; place aside. Cook all other ingredients in a separate pot for approximately 10 minutes. Cool mixture and pour over previously cooked carrots. Cover and refrigerate.

Carrot Chocolate Chip Loaf

All purpose flour	3 cups	750 ml
Sugar	1 cup	250 ml
Brown sugar	1 cup	250 ml
Ground cinnamon	2 1/2 tsp	12 ml
Baking powder	2 tsp	10 ml
Baking soda	1 tsp	5 ml
Salt	1 tsp	5 ml
Allspice	1 tsp	5 ml
Eggs	3	3
Orange juice	3/4 cup	175 ml
Vegetable oil	3/4 cup	175 ml
Vanilla extract	1 tsp	5 ml
Grated carrots	2 cups	500 ml
Semi sweet choc. chips	1 cup	250 ml

In a large bowl combine the first eight ingedients. In a small bowl, beat the eggs, orange juice, oil and vanilla. Stir into the dry ingredients just until moistened. Fold in the carrots and chocolate chips.

Transfer to two greased 8 x 4 x 2 inch loaf pans. Bake at 350° for 55-60 minutes or until a cake tester comes out clean. Cool for 10 minutes; remove from pans to wire racks.

See photo page 56.

Hint! Fastest, tastiest carrots ever! Open a can of peach pie filling and stir over cooked, sliced carrots.

Hidden Surprise Carrot Cake

Eggs	3	3
Sugar	1 3/4 cups	425 ml
Shredded carrots	3 cups	750 ml
Vegetable oil	1 cup	250 ml
All purpose flour	2 cups	500 ml
Baking soda	2 tsp	10 ml
Ground cinnamon	2 tsp	10 ml
Allspice	1 tsp	5 ml
Cloves	1/2 tsp	2 ml
Salt	1 tsp	5 ml
Chopped pecans	1/2 cup	125 ml

FILLING:

Cream cheese	8 oz pkg	250 g pkg
Sugar	1/4 cup	60 ml
Egg	1	1
Grated orange rind	2 tsp	10 ml

FROSTING:

Cream cheese	8 oz pkg	250 g pkg
Butter	1/4 cup	60 ml
Vanilla extract	2 tsp	10 ml
Confectioners sugar	4 cups	1000 ml
Grated orange rind	2 tsp	10 ml

In a mixing bowl, beat eggs and sugar. Add carrots and oil; beat until blended. Combine the flour, baking soda, spices and salt. Add to carrot mixture; mix well. Stir in pecans. Pour 3 cups of batter into a greased and floured 10 inch fluted tube pan. In a mixing bowl, beat cream cheese, sugar and orange rind. Add egg; mix well. Spoon over batter. Top with remaining batter.

Bake at 350° for 55-60 minutes or until a cake tester inserted near the centre comes out clean. Cool for 10 minutes before removing from pan to a wire rack to cool completely.

For frosting, in a small mixing bowl, beat the cream cheese, orange rind, butter and vanilla until smooth. Gradually add confectioners sugar. Frost cake. Store in the refrigerator. Makes 12-16 servings and won't your guests be surprised when they find that ribbon of cream cheese filling in every piece you serve!

See photo page 92.

Hint! Dry weather early in the summer encourages carrots to produce longer roots, so don't water during this period.

35

Carrot and Pineapple Muffins

Sifted flour	1 1/2 cups	375 ml
Sugar	1 cup	250 ml
Baking powder	1 tsp	5 ml
Baking soda	1 tsp	5 ml
Cinnamon	1 tsp	5 ml
Salt	1/2 tsp	2 ml
Salad oil	2/3 cup	150 ml
Eggs	2	2
Grated raw carrot	1 cup	250 ml
Crushed pineapple	1/2 cup	125 ml
Vanilla	1 tsp	5 ml

Put flour, sugar, baking powder, baking soda, cinnamon and salt in bowl. Add oil, eggs, carrot, pineapple (with juice) and vanilla. Blend on low speed to moisten; then beat 2 minutes at medium speed. Put in muffin pans. Bake at 325° for approximately 25 minutes. Makes about 20 muffins.

See photo page 91.

Family Supper

1. Raspberry Orange Swirls, page 116
2. Orange Chicken
3. Corn with Spicy Corn Spread, page 44
4. Bacon/Chive Potato Patties, page 78
5. Apple Glazed Carrots, page 148

Flower arrangement:

Scentimental (floribunda rose) alng with an assortment of Parkland Roses.

Carrot Burgers

Diced carrots	1 1/2 cups	375 ml
Crushed Honey Nut cornflakes	2 cups	500 ml
Eggs	2	2
Diced green pepper	1/4 cup	60 ml
Chopped onion	1 tbsp	15 ml
Salt	1/2 tsp	2 ml
Pepper	1/2 tsp	2 ml
Sugar	1/4 tsp	1 ml
Oil	2 tbsp	30 ml

Cook carrots in water first until tender; drain. In a bowl combine carrots, honeynut cornflakes, eggs, pepper, onion and seasonings. Mix well.

Form into 6 patties. Heat oil in frying pan and cook patties over medium heat on each side until browned.

Serve as a side dish or on buns.

Bits and Bites

1. Creamy Vegetable Dip, page 142
2. Curry Dip, page 138
3. Carrot Dip, page 140
4. Cucumber Canapes, page 47
5. Asparagus Rolls, page 9
6. Tomato Basil Squares, page 96
7. Decorative Radish Mice
8. Tomato Salad Cups, page 99

Flower arrangement:

Gypsophila 'Snowflake', Zinnia, Calendula.

Missouri Soup

Diced carrots	1 cup	250 ml
Diced celery	1 cup	250 ml
Diced potatoes	1 1/4 cups	310 ml
Diced onions	1/2 cup	125 ml
Broccoli	2 cups	500 ml
Cauliflower	2 cups	500 ml
Cream of chicken soup	2 cans	2 cans
Velveeta cheese	1 lb	450 g

Boil first 4 ingredients in 6 cups of hot water. In another pot, boil cauliflower and broccoli florets until tender. Drain. Add broccoli and cauliflower to other vegetable mixture. Boil for 20 minutes longer. Add 2 cans of soup and Velveeta cheese.

Keep hot, stirring frequently until cheese has melted. Do not boil. Mash with vegetable masher. Soup can be puréed in a blender for a smoother texture, if preferred.

This soup freezes well.

Faye's Mom's Super Cauliflower

Cauliflower	1 head	1 head
Sloppy Joe mix	1 envelope	1 envelope
Bread crumbs	1/4 cup	60 ml
Melted butter	1 tbsp	15 ml
Sour cream	1/2 cup	125 ml
Mayonnaise	1/4 cup	60 ml
Milk	2 tbsp	30 ml

Cut cauliflower into florets. Cook cauliflower until crisp tender. Spoon into casserole. In a bowl, combine 1 tbsp of Sloppy Joe mix with bread crumbs and butter. In a separate bowl, combine remaining Sloppy Joe mix, sour cream, mayonnaise and milk. Spoon this over cauliflower, then top with crumb mixture.

Bake at 350° for 35 to 40 minutes.

Hint! *To get white cauliflower, tie the leaves up over the head to keep light from getting at the curd.*

Turk's Dish

Cauliflower	1 head	1 head
Potatoes	4-5 med	4-5 med
Ground beef	1 lb	500 g
Hollandaise Sauce	2 pkgs	2 pkgs

Break cauliflower into medium sized florets. Boil, peel and mash potatoes. Line the bottom of a 9 x 13 inch greased pan with mashed potatoes. Brown the ground beef and layer over potatoes. Steam or boil the cauliflower until it starts to soften (just enough so a fork can pierce the pieces). Layer cauliflower over meat.

Make Hollandaise sauce (package instructions) and pour over the top. The sauce drips down through the meat as well. Bake at 350° until cauliflower begins to brown (approximately 30 minutes but time will vary depending on oven).

If you wish to make your own Hollandaise Sauce, place 1/2 cup cold milk, 4 egg yolks and the juice of 2 lemons in a small saucepan. Pan and ingredients should be cold to start. Cook, stirring over low heat and at no time allow sauce to boil. Remove from heat if necessary and continue stirring. Requires about 5-6 minutes cooking time.

Summer Savoury Cauliflower Pie

Crushed herb and garlic croutons	3 cups	750 ml
Butter	1/2 cup	125 ml
Cauliflower	5 cups	1000 ml
Chopped onion	1/2 cup	125 ml
Grated zucchini	1/2 cup	125 ml
Minced garlic	1 clove	1 clove
Salt	1/2 tsp	2 ml
Dried oregano	1/4-1/2 tsp	1-2 ml
Shredded cheddar cheese	1 cup	125 ml
Eggs	2	2
Milk	1/4 cup	125 ml

In a bowl, combine croutons and 1/4 cup butter. Press onto the bottom and up the sides of an ungreased 9 inch pie plate. Bake at 375° for 8 minutes or until lightly browned; set aside.

In a large skillet, sauté the cauliflower, onion, zucchini, garlic, salt and oregano in the remaining butter over medium heat for 10 minutes, stirring frequently. Sprinkle 1/2 cup cheese into prepared crust. Top with cauliflower mixture and remaining cheese. In a bowl, beat the eggs and milk. Pour over pie.

Bake, uncovered at 375° for 30 minutes or until a knife inserted near center comes out clean and cauliflower is tender.
Makes 6-8 servings.

Waldorf Salad

Large apples	2-3	2-3
Chopped celery	1/2-3/4 cup	125-175 ml
Chopped walnuts	1/3 cup	75 ml
Green grapes	1/4 cup	60 ml
Salad dressing	1/3 cup	75 ml
Lemon juice	1-2 tbsp	15-30 ml
Milk	1 tbsp	15 ml

Peel and dice apples. Combine all ingredients immediately to prevent apples from browning. Refrigerate.

Cream of Celery Soup

Butter	1 tbsp	15 ml
Chopped celery	1 - 11/2 cups	250-375 ml
Sliced onions	1/3 cup	75 ml
Poultry stock*	2 cups	500 ml
Milk	1 1/2 cups	375 ml
Cornstarch	1 1/2 tbsp	22.5 ml
Cold milk	1/2 cup	125 ml
Chopped dill	2 tsp	10 ml

* Poultry stock: 4 tsp chicken bouillion powder with 2 cups boiling water.

Melt 1 tbsp butter. Add and sauté celery (including leaves) and onions for 2 minutes. Pour in poultry stock and simmer about 10 minutes.
Strain the soup. Add 1 1/2 cups milk and bring to the boiling point.
In another small bowl dissolve 1 1/2 tbsp cornstarch in 1/2 cup cold milk. Stir this mixture gradually into the hot soup. Bring to a boil. Stir and simmer about 1 minute. Garnish with chopped dill or parsley if you prefer.

Hint! To restore crispness to celery, place in cold water, add a slice of raw potato, let stand a few hours.

Corn Chowder

Fresh corn	4 ears	4 ears
Water	1 cup	250 ml
Cubed potatoes	1/2 cup	125 ml
Chopped onions	1 med	1 med
Chopped celery	1 stalk	1 stalk
Chicken bouillion	4 tsp	20 ml
Milk	1 3/4 cups	425 ml
Butter	1 tbsp	15 ml
Flour	2-3 tbsp	30-45 ml
Crisp crumbled bacon	4 slices	4 slices
Parsley	1 tbsp	15 ml
Salt	to taste	to taste
Pepper	to taste	to taste

Remove corn husks; scrub with stiff brush to remove silk. Rinse. Use a sharp knife to cut off just the kernel tips. Then scrape cobs with dull edge of knife (about 2 cups).

In a large saucepan combine corn, water, potato, onion, celery, bouillion and 1/4 tsp pepper. Bring to a boil. Reduce heat. Cover; simmer about 10 minutes until corn and potatoes are just tender stirring occasionally. Stir in 1 1/2 cups of milk and the butter.

Gradually stir rest of milk into the flour, stir into corn mixture. Cook and stir for 1 minute more. Season with salt and pepper. Serve in bowls. Sprinkle crumbled bacon and parsley on top of each serving.

See photo page 55.

Corn with Savoury Lime Butter

Fresh corn	8 ears	8 ears
Softened butter	1/2 cup	125 ml
Dried savoury	3/4 tsp	3 ml
Salt	to taste	to taste
Shredded lime peel	1 tsp	5 ml

Remove husks and silks. Rinse. In a large Dutch oven cook corn uncovered for 5-7 minutes (until tender), in enough lightly sugared water to cover. In a small bowl thoroughly combine butter, savoury, salt and lime peel. Spread on piping hot corn.

Hint!   To microwave corn on the cob, place 1-5 ears with husks in a casserole dish and cover. Cook 3-4 minutes per ear depending on wattage. Rinse after cooking with warm water and remove husks and silk.

Spicy Corn Spread

Softened butter	1/4 cup	60 ml
Parsley flakes	1/2 tsp	2 ml
Salt	1/4 tsp	1 ml
Pepper	1/4 tsp	1 ml
Chili powder	1/4 tsp	1 ml

Mix all ingredients together in a small bowl, spread on freshly cooked corn.

See photo page 37.

Salmon Corn Chowder

Cubed potatoes	2 cups	500 ml
Fresh corn	1 1/2 cups	375 ml
Chopped onion	1 med	1 med
Grated carrot	1 med	1 med
Chicken broth	1 can	1 can
Boneless salmon steak	1 lb	500 g
Crisp crumbled bacon	1/2 lb	250 g
Milk	2 cups	500 ml
Blend cream	1 cup	250 ml
Butter	1 tbsp	15 ml
Salt	to taste	to taste
Pepper	to taste	to taste
Tarragon	to taste	to taste

Bring potatoes, corn, onion, carrots and broth to a boil in a large pot. Reduce heat, cover and cook until potatoes are tender. Add salmon and bacon, cook until salmon flakes easily.

Reduce heat, stir in milk, blend cream, butter and seasonings. Heat but do not boil. Thicken if desired.

Sweet Corn Toss

Cooked corn cobs	2 ears	2 ears
Chopped red pepper	1	1
Sliced green onions	2	2
Italian dressing	1/4 cup	60 ml

Slice kernels from cob, mix with remaining ingredients. Serve.

Hint! When boiling corn on the cob in water, do not add salt as this toughens the corn. Use sugar or a splash of milk which will help sweeten the corn.

Roasted Corn and Garlic Rice

Fresh corn	4 ears	4 ears
Garlic cloves	2	2
Long grain rice uncooked	1 cup	250 ml
Chicken broth	2 cups	500 ml
Salt	1/4 tsp	1 ml
Pepper	to taste	to taste
Olive oil	2 1/4 tsp	11 ml

Peel back husks from corn to within one inch from bottom, remove silk. Rewrap in husks.

Place peeled garlic cloves on heavy duty foil, drizzle with 1/4 tsp olive oil.

Fold foil around garlic, seal tightly. Place corn and garlic on oven rack, bake at 400° for 30 minutes. Remove corn, bake garlic for another 10 minutes. Remove garlic, place in bowl, cool, mash.

Remove corn from cobs with a knife.

In a saucepan, heat 2 tsp olive oil, add rice, cook 2 minutes. Add broth and seasonings and garlic. Bring to a boil. Reduce heat, cover and cook 13 minutes. Stir in corn, cook 10 minutes longer.

Succotash

Chopped onion	1 med	1 med
Butter	2 oz	80 g
Finely chopped onion	1 sm	1 sm
Chopped bacon	1 strip	1 strip
Fresh corn kernels	2 cups	500 ml
Chopped red pepper	1 cup	250 ml
Frozen broad beans	1 lb	500 g
Cream	1/4 cup	60 ml

Heat butter in large pan; cook onion, bacon, corn and red pepper, stirring, about 5 minutes or until corn is tender. Add remaining ingredients, stir until heated through. Best served the day it's made. Serves 6.

Hint! Corn is wind pollinated, so plant it in blocks as opposed to long rows to ensure good pollination.

Crunchy Cuke Rounds

Cucumbers	3	3
Chopped red apple	1 cup	250 ml
Unsweetened crushed pineapple	1 can	1 can
Toasted, chopped pecans	1/4 cup	60 ml
Low fat sour cream	1/4 cup	60 ml
Salt	1/8 tsp	.5 ml

In a small bowl, combine the apple, pineapple, pecans, sour cream and salt. Cover and refrigerate until chilled. To score cucumbers, cut lengthwise strips through peel. Cut each cucumber into 16 slices. Blot with paper towels to remove moisture. Spoon 1 teaspoon apple mixture onto each slice. Makes 4 dozen appetizers.

Alice's Lime Cucumber Salad

Lime jello	1 lg pkg	1 lg pkg
Diced, peeled cucumber	1 cup	250 ml
Crushed pineapple	14 oz	420 g
Cottage cheese	1 cup	250 ml
Miracle Whip	1 cup	250 ml

Dissolve jello in 2 cups of hot water and 1 cup cold water (or pineapple juice). Pour 1/4 - 1/2 cup into mold(s) until partially set. When unmolded, the top will be bright green, the rest a lighter creamy green.

In a bowl, add the pineapple juice (or a combination of pineapple juice and water to equal 1 cup), to the remaining liquid jello. Set partially in fridge. Add pineapple, cucumber, cottage cheese and Miracle Whip to the partially set jello in the bowl. Mix well.

Finally, add this mixture carefully to the partially set jello that is already in the mold(s), so it isn't disturbed. Place in fridge to set for several hours. Loosen edges of molded salad with knife. Turn out onto serving plate when ready to serve.

See photo page 74.

Hint! If starting cucumbers indoors be sure and use pots that can be planted directly into the ground to protect their delicate roots.

Mustard Pickles

White sugar	7 cups	1750 ml
White vinegar	4 cups	1000 ml
Pickling salt	4 tbsp	60 ml
Flour	1 1/2 cups	375 ml
Mustard seed	2 tbsp	30 ml
Turmeric	1 tbsp	15 ml
Dry mustard	2 tbsp	30 ml
Pepper	1 tsp	5 ml
Cauliflower	1	1
Chopped onions	3 lbs	1.5 kg
Cucumbers	12 med	12 med
Red pepper	2	2
Green pepper	1	1

Mix first 8 ingredients together until smooth.

Dice cucumbers; cut cauliflower into small florets; chop peppers into small pieces. In a large saucepan, mix all vegetables together. Drain off any liquid from vegetables.

Pour dressing over vegetables and cook, stirring, until sauce is thick. Keep a close watch and stir often, keeping contents just to the boil. Turn off heat. Bottle and seal in Mason jars.

Option: *You may substitute an equal amount of silverskinned onions in brine for regular onions.*

See photo page 128.

Cucumber Canapes

Cucumber	1	1
Water	1 cup	250 ml
Cider vinegar	1/2 cup	125 ml
Smoked salmon flavoured		
cream cheese	1 pkg	1 pkg
Bread slices	36	36
Stuffed olives	36	36

With a fork, score cucumber lengthwise; cut into thin slices. Place in a bowl; add water and vinegar. Let stand for 30 minutes. Meanwhile, in a small bowl, beat flavoured cream cheese.

Cut bread into flower shapes with a 2 1/2 inch cookie cutter. Spread each with cream cheese mixture; top with a cucumber slice. Remove pimentos from olives; place in center of cucumber. Cut olives into 5 wedges and arrange around pimiento in a pinwheel pattern.

See photo page 38.

Hint! If you need to remove the seeds easily, cut the cucumber in half lengthwise, run a melon baller down the length to remove seeds.

47

Cucumber Veggie Salad

Cucumbers	4 cups	1000 ml
Chopped celery	1 cup	250 ml
Chopped onion	1/4 cup	60 ml
Green pepper	1/8 cup	30 ml
Red pepper	1/8 cup	30 ml
Sugar	1/4 cup	60 ml
Vinegar	1/4 cup	60 ml
Oil	2 tbsp	30 ml
Celery seeds	to taste	to taste
Salt	to taste	to taste
Pepper	to taste	to taste

Peel and slice cucumbers; combine vegetables in a medium bowl. Bring sugar, vinegar, oil and seasonings to a boil. Pour over vegetables. Refrigerate for 2 hours or up to 2 days

Eggplant Bake

Eggplant	1 lb	500 g
Tomato	1 large	1 large
Onion	1 med	1 med
Melted butter	6 tbsp	90 ml
Dried basil	1/2 tsp	2 ml
Dry bread crumbs	1/2 cup	125 ml
Mozzarella cheese	1 cup	250 ml
Parmesan cheese	2 tbsp	30 ml

Peel and cut eggplant into 1/2 inch slices. Place eggplant slices in a colander over a plate. Sprinkle with salt; toss. Let stand 30 minutes. Rinse and drain well.

Layer the eggplant, tomato and onion in a lightly greased 13 x 9 x 2 inch baking dish. Drizzle with 4 tbsp butter; sprinkle with basil. Cover and bake at 450° for 20 minutes.

Toss the bread crumbs and remaining butter. Arrange shredded mozarella cheese over vegetables; sprinkle with crumb mixture and parmesan cheese. Bake uncovered for 10 minutes or until cheese is bubbly. Makes 6 servings.

See photo page 128.

Stuffed Eggplant

Eggplants	4 med	4 med
Onions	2 med	2 med
Tomatoes	1 1/4 lbs	625 g
Olive oil	3 tbsp	45 ml
Garlic cloves	2	2
Salt	to taste	to taste
Fresh ground pepper	to taste	to taste
Chopped parsley	1 tbsp	15 ml
Bread cubes	1 1/2 cups	375 ml
Melted butter	2 tbsp	30 ml

Roast the eggplants in a preheated oven at 400° for about 10 minutes, turning frequently. Pull off the skins, halve the eggplants lengthwise, carefully scoop out and reserve most of the flesh, leaving a 3/4 inch thick shell. Slice the onions and separate into rings. Peel, quarter, seed and dice the tomatoes. Heat 2 tsp of the olive oil in a saucepan and sauté the onions and garlic. Add the tomatoes. Season with salt and pepper and cook for 5 minutes.

Coarsely dice the eggplant flesh, add to the saucepan and cook for a further 5 minutes. Add the parsley. Use this mixture to stuff the eggplant shells. Arrange the stuffed eggplants in an oiled casserole and drizzle with the remaining oil.

In a separate bowl, toss and coat the bread cubes with melted butter. Add buttered cubes to top of shells. Bake in a preheated oven at 350° for 15-20 minutes or until the eggplant shells are tender.

Eggplant Pockets

Sliced eggplant	12 slices	12 slices
Bread crumbs	3/4 cup	175 ml
Grated Parmesan	1/2 cup	125 ml
Chopped plum tomatoes	1/2 cup	125 ml
Olive oil	1/4 cup	60 ml
Parsley	2 tbsp	30 ml
Minced garlic	1 clove	1 clove
Salt	1/2 tsp	2 ml
Pepper	1/4 tsp	1 ml

Slice eggplant into slices 1/4 inch thick and 3 inches wide. Combine bread crumbs, cheese, tomato, 2 tbsp of the oil, parsley, garlic, 1/4 tsp of the salt and pepper; set aside. Brush both sides of eggplant with remaining oil; sprinkle with remaining salt. Arrange half the slices on baking sheet; top evenly with bread crumb mixture. Sandwich with remaining slices.

Bake at 450° turning once, for about 20 minutes or until brown. Makes 6 servings.

Eggplant Parmesan

Eggplant	1 large	1 large
Parmesan cheese	1/2 cup	125 ml
Grated mozzarella	3/4 cup	175 ml
Grated cheddar	3/4 cup	175 ml
Cottage cheese	1 cup	250 ml
Herb/Garlic flavoured olive oil	1-2 tbsp	15-30 ml
LAYER SAUCE		
Chopped onion	1/2 cup	125 ml
Chopped green pepper	1/2 cup	125 ml
Grated carrot	1/2 cup	125 ml
Olive oil	4 tbsp	60 ml
Tomatoes	19 oz can	600 g
Tomato paste	5 1/2 oz can	150 g
Oregano	to taste	to taste
Garlic powder	to taste	to taste
Thyme	to taste	to taste
Salt	to taste	to taste

Slice eggplant, brush with herb and garlic flavoured olive oil and broil on both sides until soft. Cover with grated Parmesan cheese.

Combine the Layer Sauce ingredients, cook for 20 minutes. Using a 9 x 13 inch greased casserole, layer the eggplant slices, the grated cheeses, the cottage cheese, sauce, etc.

Bake at 350° for 40 minutes. Serves 6.

Eggplant French Fries

Dry bread crumbs	2/3 cup	150 ml
Parmesan cheese	1/2 cup	125 ml
Parsley	1/2 tsp	2 ml
Poultry seasoning	1/4 tsp	1 ml
Onion powder	1/4 tsp	1 ml
Salt	dash	dash
Pepper	dash	dash
Eggplant	1 large	1 large
Ranch salad dressing	2/3 cup	150 ml

Peel and cut eggplant into french fry sized pieces. Stir all ingredients together except the eggplant and salad dressing. Dip eggplant pieces into salad dressing; coat well. Roll pieces in dry crumb mixture. Place pieces on a greased baking sheet; bake at 400° for 12-15 minutes or until browned. Serve immediately.

Kale and Squash Pie

Pine nuts	1/4 cup	60 ml
Kale	1/2 bunch	.5 bunch
Olive oil	2 tbsp	30 ml
Chopped green onions	6	6
Salt	3/4 tsp	3 ml
Pepper	3/4 tsp	3 ml
Chopped onion	1 med	1 med
Butternut squash, cubed	4 cups	1000 ml
Dried sage, crumbled	1/2 tsp	2 ml
Grated Parmesan	1/2 cup	125 ml
Dry bread crumbs	2 tbsp	30 ml
Chopped parsley	2 tbsp	30 ml
Phyllo pastry	8	8
Melted butter	1/2 cup	125 ml

In a small skillet, toast pine nuts over medium low heat until light brown, about 8 minutes.

On cutting board, trim off stems and centre ribs of kale; discard. Coarsley chop leaves to make 12 cups. Set aside.

In large skillet, heat half of the oil over medium heat; fry green onions, salt and pepper until softened, about 5 minutes.

Add half of the chopped kale and 1/2 cup water; cook, stirring until slightly wilted, about 1 minute. Add remaining kale; cook, stirring frequently, until tender and liquid is evaporated, about 10 minutes. Stir in toasted pine nuts. Set aside.

In large skillet, heat remaining oil over medium heat; fry chopped onion with, salt and pepper, stirring occasionally, until softened, about 5 minutes.

Add squash and sage; fry until squash is tender, about 8 minutes. Stir in parmesan cheese, bread crumbs and parsley. let cool.

Lightly butter 9 inch spring form pan. Lightly brush 1 sheet of phyllo with butter, keeping remaining phyllo covered with damp towel to prevent drying out. Line up short end of phyllo sheet with center of pan and lay in pan, fitting over bottom and up sides and leaving overhang.

Lay second sheet of buttered phyllo next to but generously overlapping first sheet. Repeat with remaining 6 sheets of phyllo, overlapping each to cover bottom of pan. Spoon in half of the kale mixture; top with squash mixture and remaining kale. Fold phyllo overhang over filling; brush top with butter and tuck in edge.

Bake at 400° until crispy and golden brown, about 25 minutes. Let pie cool on rack for 10 minutes before cutting.

Makes 8 servings.

Scottish Leek Broth

Cubed ham	1-1 1/2 lbs	500-750 g
Split peas	3 cups	750 ml
Barley	3 cups	750 ml
Dried peas	3 cups	750 ml
Diced carrots	3 lbs	1.5 kg
Diced turnip	1 med	1 med
Diced parsnip	1 med	1 med
Chopped leeks	2 lbs	1 kg
Finely grated carrot	1 med	1 med
Baking soda	2 tsp	10 ml

Boil split peas, barley and dried peas with baking soda. Let stand overnight and wash well the next day. Strain stock. Put stock in large pot and add all ingredients (except leeks) and boil gently for one hour. Add leeks, cook an additional 10 minutes. Finely grate a carrot for top.

Pork Chops and Leeks

Olive oil	2 tbsp	30 ml
Chopped onion	1/2	.5
Diced red pepper	1	1
Chicken broth	2 1/2 cups	625 ml
White rice	1 cup	250 ml
Salt	1/2 tsp	2 ml
Fresh peas	2 cups	500 ml
Trimmed leeks	3	3
Rib pork chops	4	4
Black pepper	1/8 tsp	.5 ml
White wine	1/3 cup	75 ml

In a medium sized saucepan, heat 1 tbsp of oil over medium heat. Add onion and red pepper. Cook, stirring for 5 minutes. Add broth, rice and 1/4 tsp of salt. Bring to a boil. Reduce to low. Cover; simmer for 17-20 minutes, adding peas for last 5 minutes, until rice is tender.

Meanwhile, cut leeks in half lengthwise; pull apart and rinse under cool water to remove any soil. Cut crosswise into 1/2 inch pieces. Season pork chops with remaining salt and pepper. Heat remaining oil in a large non-stick skillet over medium heat. Sauté chops 2 minutes per side. Remove.

In the same skillet sauté leeks for 5 minutes, stirring occasionally. Add wine and chops. Cover, simmer 5 minutes until internal temperature of pork registers 155°. Serve chops topped with leek mixture and rice pilaf on the side.

Leek and Potato Soup

Oil	1 tbsp	15 ml
Chopped onion	1 med	1 med
Finely sliced potatoes	10-12 med	10-12 med
Sliced leeks (white only)	3	3
Stock	1 qt	1.1 lit
Salt and Pepper	to taste	to taste
Diced salt pork	1 tbsp	15 ml
Diced carrot	1 med	1 med
Diced celery	4 stalks	4 stalks
Diced zucchini	1/2 cup	125 ml
Diced turnip	1/4	1/4
Scalded cream	as needed	as need
Parsley	dash	dash

Sauté onions and leeks in oil. Add sliced potatoes and stock. Simmer until tender and purée in blender. Add scalded cream to desired texture.

Sauté salt pork and add diced vegetables except zucchini. Do not cover. Sauté 5 minutes. Add zucchini and simmer another 5 minutes. Add to hot potato/leek mixture; season to taste and garnish with chopped parsley.

Leek, Egg and Cheese Strata

Olive oil	2 tbsp	30 ml
Leeks without leaves	6	6
Salt and pepper	to taste	to taste
Whole wheat bread	8-12 slices	8-12 slices
Grated cheddar	2 cups	500 ml
Grated Monterey Jack	1 cup	250 ml
Dijon mustard	1 tbsp	15 ml
Eggs	6	6
Blend cream (10%)	3 cups	750 ml

Sauté leeks in oil for 5 minutes. Add seasonings. Remove from heat.

Cover bottom of 13 x 9 x 2 inch baking dish with a layer of bread slices, cutting them to fit if necessary. Top with half the leeks and half of the cheese. Repeat layers once.

Whisk mustard, eggs and blend cream. Season with salt and pepper. Pour over bread. Let sit for at least one hour or overnight in fridge.

Bake at 350° for 40 minutes. Cool slightly before cutting.

Hint! When transplanting leeks, put them in a hole 4-5 inches deep to help blanch the stem.

Three Green Salad

Iceberg lettuce	4 cups	1000 ml
Leaf lettuce	4 cups	1000 ml
Mesclun mix	4 cups	1000 ml
Sliced cucumber	1 med	1 med
Sliced carrots	2 med	2 med
Sliced celery ribs	2 stalks	2 stalks
Broccoli florets	6-8 florets	6-8 florets
Sliced cauliflower	3 florets	3 florets
Sliced radishes	6	6
Sliced green onions	4	4
Sliced mushrooms	5 lg	5 lg

In a large salad bowl, toss the greens and vegetables. Cover and chill. For a great dressing choice try the Green Salad Dressing found on page 135.

See photo front cover.

Autumn Comfort

1. Saturday Night Baked Beans, page 11
2. Zucchini Meatball Stew, page 103
3. Corn Chowder, page 43
4. Cream of Carrot Soup, page 33
5. Island Potato Bannock, page 79

Flowers:

Ruby Eclipse Sunflower, Rudbeckia Chocolate Orange, Cherokee Sunset Rudbeckia, Hemerocallis (daylily).

Okra, Wax Bean Salad

Trimmed okra	12 oz	375 g
Yellow beans	1 lb	500 g
Mayonnaise	3 tbsp	45 ml
Red onion strips	3/4 cup	175 ml
Light sour cream	2 tbsp	30 ml
Cider vinegar	2 tbsp	30 ml
Chopped fresh dill	2 tbsp	30 ml
Prepared mustard	1 tsp	5 ml
Salt	1/2 tsp	2 ml
Pepper	1/4 tsp	1 ml
Plum tomatoes	4	4
Hard cooked egg	1	1
Crumbled bacon	4 slices	4 slices

Bring a large pot of salted water to a boil; add okra and cook 2 minutes. Remove with slotted spoon to colander; refresh under cold water. Add beans to boiling water; cook 2 to 3 minutes, or until crisp tender. Add to okra in colander and cool under cold water; drain.

Whisk mayonnaise, red onion, sour cream, vinegar, dill, mustard, salt and pepper in a large bowl; add okra and beans; toss. Stir in tomatoes after slicing them into 2 inch strips.

Cover; refrigerate at least 4 hours or overnight to allow flavours to blend. To serve, garnish with chopped egg and bacon crumbs.
Serves 8.

Afternoon Delight

1. Carrot Chocolate Chip Loaf, page 34
2. Pumpkin Bread (raisins), page 85
3. Pumpkin Bread (choc chips), page 85
4. Lemon Blueberry Scones, page 113
5. Sweet Potato Quick Bread, page 82

Flower arrangement:

Bachelor's Buttons, Dianthus 'Corona Cherry Magic', Gypsophila 'Snowflake'.

Onion Chicken Fried Rice

Rice	1 1/2 cups	375 ml
Diced tomatoes	1-2 lg	1-2 lg
Eggs	4	4
Chopped onions	4 lg	4 lg
Celery	2 stalks	2 stalks
Soya Sauce	to taste	to taste
Chopped chicken	1-1 1/2 cups	250-375 ml

In preparation for this recipe, cook 1 1/2 cups of rice (according to package directions), which should yield 3 cups and put aside. Also, chop 1-1 1/2 cups of precooked chicken and put aside.

Sauté in oil, finely chopped onions and celery. Remove from saucepan and place in casserole dish.

Fry 4 eggs, break yolks then shred and place in casserole dish. Next, fry the precooked rice with soya sauce (to taste) and also add to casserole. Just prior to serving add one or two diced tomatoes and the chopped chicken.

Keep dish warm in oven and toss prior to serving.

Onion Spread

Chopped onions	2 sm	2 sm
Mayonnaise	1/2 cups	125 ml
Ranch dressing	1/2 cup	125 ml
Monterey Jack	1 cup	250 ml
Assorted crackers	as required	as required

In a large bowl combine finely chopped onions, mayonnaise, dressing and shredded cheese. Spoon into an ungreased 9 inch pie plate. Bake, uncovered at 350° for 25-30 minutes. Broil 6 inches from the heat for 2-3 minutes or until bubbly. Serve with crackers.

A simple yet delicious appetizer.

Onion and Apple Casserole

Onions	6 med	6 med
Apples	4 med	4 med
Flour	3 tbsp	45 ml
Brown sugar	2 tbsp	30 ml
Salt	2 tsp	10 ml
Butter	as required	as required

Peel and slice onions thinly. Wash, core, peel and slice apples; toss in flour-sugar-salt mixture and arrange with onions in alternate layers in greased baking dish. Dot with butter. Cover and bake in moderate oven at 350° for 30 minutes or until tender. Uncover and brown if desired.

Makes 4 to 5 servings.

Creamed Onions

Sliced onions	6 lg	6 lg
Butter	1 cup	250 ml
Flour	2 tbsp	30 ml
Salt	2 tsp	10 ml
Pepper	1/2 tsp	2 ml
Milk	2 cups	500 ml

In a large skillet or Dutch oven, sauté sliced onions in butter until tender and golden brown, about 25 minutes. Remove with a slotted spoon and keep aside in a bowl. Add flour, salt and pepper to the skillet; stir until smooth. Gradually stir in milk until blended.

Bring to a boil, cook and stir for 2 minutes or until thickened. Reduce heat to medium. Return onions to the skillet and heat throughout. Spoon contents from skillet into a casserole dish and top with your favourite crumb topping. Bake at 350° until topping turns a golden brown.

Sample Crumb topping:

Combine 1/2 cup dry bread crumbs, 1 tbsp melted butter and 1 tbsp of parmesan cheese in a medium bowl. Toss until crumbs are coated.

Hint! Onions starting from transplants or sown from seed directly will be larger and have better shape than those from sets.

59

Caramelized Onions

Onions	4 lg	4 lg
Vegetable oil	1/4 cup	60 ml
Cider vinegar	3 tbsp	45 ml
Brown sugar	2 tbsp	30 ml

In a large skillet, sauté thinly sliced onions in oil over medium heat until tender, about 15 minutes. Stir in vinegar and brown sugar. Cook 10 minutes longer or until onions are golden.

Makes 4 to 6 servings.

Onion and Cheese Tarts

PIE DOUGH:

Flour	1 cup	250 ml
Salt	1/4 tsp	1 ml
Butter	1/3 cup	75 ml
Water	1-2 tbsp	15-30 ml

FILLING:

Beaten egg	1	1
Light cream	1/3-1/2 cup	75-125 ml
Monterey Jack	1/2 cup	125 ml
Green onions	3	3
Salt	to taste	to taste
Cayenne pepper	to taste	to taste

To make the pie dough, sift the flour and salt into a mixing bowl. Rub in the butter with your fingers until well combined and the mixture resembles fine breadcrumbs. Gradually stir in the water, adding little by little, and mix to form a smooth dough.

Roll out the pie dough on a lightly floured surface. Using a 3 inch cookie cutter, stamp out 12 rounds from the dough and line a muffin pan.

To make the filling, whisk together the beaten egg, light cream, grated Monterey Jack and chopped green onions. Season to taste with salt and cayenne.

Pour the filling mixture into the pie shells and bake in a preheated oven at 350° for about 20-25 minutes, or until the filling is just set.

Serve the tarts warm or cold.

See photo page 145.

Chop Suey

Fresh mushrooms	1 cup	250 ml
Green pepper	1 lg	1 lg
Red pepper	1 lg	1 lg
Stewing beef	1/2-1 lb	250-500 g
Onions	3	3
Bean sprouts	2 sm cans	2 sm cans
Bamboo shoots	1 can	1 can
Soya sauce	2 tbsp	30 ml
Cornstarch	to thicken	to thicken
Celery	3 stalks	3 stalks

Sauté sliced mushrooms in 2 tbsp butter. Place in casserole dish. Cut beef into small pieces and sear in frying pan with three chopped onions and 2 tbsp soya sauce. Simmer.

Sauté in 1 1/2 tbsp oil, the chopped red and green peppers along with finely chopped celery. Add 2 cans of beans sprouts, 1 can bamboo shoots, 1 1/2 cups of water and cornstarch to thicken. Add this mixture to casserole at mealtime. Stir well and serve.

Oriental Vegetable Delight

Onions	4 lg	4 lg
Celery	3 stalks	3 stalks
Green pepper	1 lg	1 lg
Soya sauce	1 tbsp	15 ml
Sliced water chestnuts	1 can	1 can
Sliced bamboo shoots	1 can	1 can

Chop vegetables listed above in advance and sauté in oil in large frying pan (cut celery at a slant to give a flat effect). Sauté along with sliced water chestnuts and bamboo shoots until soft and cooked but still crunchy. Add 1 tbsp of soya sauce just before serving.

Serves 6.

Hint! For fresh parsley quickly, chop extra parsley, put in ice cube trays and cover with a small amount of water. Once frozen, transfer to resealable bag. Toss one or two cubes in soups or stews.

Sweet Roasted Parsnips/Carrots

Parsnips	12 oz	375 g
Carrots	6 med	6 med
Olive oil	1 tbsp	15 ml
Salt	1/2 tsp	2 ml
Pepper	1/4 tsp	1 ml
Maple syrup	1 tbsp	15 ml

Heat oven to 450°. Place peeled parsnip and carrots (all cut to a similar size and shape) on baking sheet. Sprinkle with oil, salt and pepper; stir gently until evenly coated.

Bake 25 to 30 minutes, turning vegetables over after 15 minutes, until tender and browned. Remove from oven, drizzle with maple syrup and gently toss until coated. Transfer to a serving bowl; serve immediately. Serves 4.

See photo page 127.

Parsnip Turnip Casserole

Diced turnip	1 med	1 med
Diced carrots	6 med	6 med
Diced parsnips	3 med	3 med
Salt	to taste	to taste
Pepper	to taste	to taste
Butter	1/4 cup	60 ml
Slightly beaten egg	1	1

Steam vegetables until cooked and mash thoroughly (or put through food processor). Add butter, salt and pepper to taste. Cool slightly and blend in egg. Pour into a well buttered casserole. Dot with butter. Bake at 375° for 35 minutes.

Hint! To roast parsnips or carrots evenly, cut thick or large vegetables lengthwise in halves or quarters.

French Parsnips

Parsnips	2 cups	500 ml
Boiling water	1/2 cup	125 ml
Butter	2 tbsp	30 ml
Sugar	1 tbsp	15 ml
Salt	1/4 tsp	1 ml
Lemon juice	1 tsp	5 ml
Parsley	garnish	garnish

Peel and grate parsnips and place in saucepan along with water, butter, sugar, salt and lemon juice. Cover pan. Simmer the parsnips until the water is absorbed.

Serve, sprinkled with chopped parsley.

Parsnip Veggie Roast

Parsnips	3	3
Carrots	3	3
New potatoes	1 lb	500 g
Turnip	2	2
Celery	6 stalks	6 stalks
Red onion	1 med	1 med
Balsamic vinegar	1/4 cup	60 ml
Olive oil	3 tbsp	45 ml
Sugar	1 tsp	5 ml
Rosemary	1 tsp	5 ml
Salt	1/2 tsp	2 ml
Pepper	1/4 tsp	1 ml

To prepare, peel and slice parsnips and carrots into 1 1/2 inch pieces; halve potatoes; peel and cut turnip into 1 inch pieces; slice celery; cut onions into wedges.

Lightly grease a 15 1/2 x 10 1/2 x 2 inch roasting pan. Combine all vegetables and place in pan. In a small mixing bowl stir together balsamic vinegar, oil, sugar, rosemary, salt and pepper. Drizzle over vegetables.

Bake, uncovered, in a 450° oven for 45-50 minutes or until potatoes and onion wedges are tender; stirring twice during baking time.

To serve, transfer vegetables to a serving dish. Makes approximately 8 servings.

Hint! To ensure a good stand of parsnips, lay a board along the row until they come up to keep the soil moist.

Parsnip Patties

Shredded parsnips	3 cups	750 ml
Slightly beaten egg	1	1
Chopped green onions	2	2
Flour	1/2 cup	125 ml
Salt	1/2 tsp	2 ml
Warmed honey	1/2 cup	125 ml

In a bowl, combine peeled, shredded parsnips, egg, onion, flour and salt. Drop batter by 1/2 cupfuls on a lightly greased hot frying pan. Fry over medium heat for 4-5 minutes per side or until vegetables are tender. Serve with honey. Makes 6 servings.

Creamed Peas On Toast

Cooked peas	1 1/2 - 2 cups	375-500 ml
Butter	1/3 cup	75 ml
Flour	1/3 cup	75 ml
Salt	3/4 tsp	3 ml
Pepper	1/8 tsp	.5 ml
Milk	1 1/2 cups	375 ml
Toasted bread	6-8 slices	6-8 slices

Melt butter in saucepan. Mix in flour, salt and pepper. Stir in milk until it boils and thickens. Add more milk if sauce becomes too thick. Add precooked peas. Stir.
Serve on toast.

Meatless Meat Loaf

Cooked rice	4 cups	1000 ml
Soya sauce	2 tbsp	30 ml
Margarine	4 tbsp	60 ml
Onions	2 tbsp	30 ml
Cooked peas	1 cup	250 ml
Scrambled eggs	4	4
Special K cereal	6 cups	1500 ml
Cottage cheese	14 oz	420 g
Beaten eggs	6	6
Dry onion soup mix	1 pkg	1 pkg
Oil	1/4 cup	60 ml

Add soya sauce to cooked rice, then set aside. Brown onion in 2 tbsp of margarine. Scramble eggs in 2 tbsp margarine and season. Mix cooked peas with half of the scrambled eggs (save remaining half of eggs for top). Mix together cereal, cottage cheese, 6 beaten eggs, onion mix and oil. Mix this with all other ingredients, except for eggs to spread over top. Bake in a 9 x 13 inch pan at 350° for one hour.

See photo page 128.

Bubble and Squeak

Potatoes	4 med	4 med
Carrots	2 med	2 med
Pumpkin	8 oz	250 g
Chopped onion	7 oz	200 g
Peas	1 cup	250 ml
Shredded cabbage	1 cup	250 ml
Butter	3 tbsp	45 ml
Vegetable oil	2 tbsp	30 ml

Boil, steam or microwave potatoes until tender; drain, mash, cool. Cut carrots and pumpkin into 1 inch pieces. Cook carrots, pumpkin, onion, peas and cabbage separately in pan of boiling water until tender; drain. Combine mashed potato with all vegetables in bowl; mix well.

Heat butter and oil in frying pan; add vegetable mixture, press down with flat spatula, cook, without stirring until brown underneath. Cut into serving slices using spatula, turn pieces over, cook until browned on other side. Serves 6

Snow Peas and Peppers

Butter	1 tbsp	15 ml
Minced garlic	2 cloves	2 cloves
Salt	1/4 tsp	1 ml
Pepper	1/4 tsp	1 ml
Sliced red pepper	1	1
Chopped snow peas	3 cups	750 ml
Wine vinegar	1 tbsp	15 ml

In a deep skillet, heat butter (or vegetable oil) over medium heat. Cook garlic, minced; and salt and pepper until fragrant, about 30 seconds. Add sliced red pepper and chopped snow peas. Cover and cook, stirring occasionally, until tender crisp, about 5 minutes. Stir in wine vinegar.
Makes 4 servings

Snow Pea Blend

Snow peas	4 cups	1000 ml
Sliced carrots	1 cup	250 ml
Sliced zucchini	1 cup	250 ml
Olive oil	2 tsp	10 ml
Cornstarch	2 tsp	10 ml
Chicken broth	1 cup	250 ml
Soy sauce	2 tsp	10 ml

In a skillet, sauté peas, carrots and sliced zucchini in oil. In a bowl, combine cornstarch, broth and soy sauce until smooth; add to vegetable mixture. Bring to a boil; cook and stir for 1-2 minutes or until thickened. Makes 6 servings

Stuffed Green Peppers

Green peppers	4-6	4-6
Salt	1 tsp	5 ml
Pepper	1/2 tsp	2 ml
Chopped onion	1 med	1 med
Lean ground beef	1 1/2 lbs	750 g
Garlic salt	1/2 tsp	2 ml
Chopped mushrooms	1 cup	250 ml
Uncooked rice	1/2 cup	125 ml
Chopped tomatoes	4 med	4 med
Melted butter	2 tbsp	30 ml
Bread crumbs	3/4 cup	175 ml
Grated cheese	1/2 cup	125 ml

Select firm green peppers. Slice a top from each. Remove stem ends. Remove seeds and membranes from peppers. Cook in boiling salted water for 5 minutes only; drain and sprinkle with salt. Let cool; place in flat casserole dish.

FILLING:

Cook 1/2 cup of your favourite uncooked rice.
In frying pan with enough oil to lightly cover bottom, sauté chopped onions and add ground beef; brown lightly, add salt , freshly ground pepper and garlic salt to taste.
When chopping tomatoes, reserve juices. Add chopped tomatoes into meat mixture and add sliced and chopped fresh mushrooms, along with cooked rice.
Mix all in pan and taste for flavour. Use enough of the mixture to fill peppers. Pour any reserved tomato juice over the filled peppers. Place tops on peppers. Place any leftover filling on the bottom of the flat casserole dish. Place filled peppers on top of the extra filling. Do not cover. Bake at 350° for approximately 20-30 minutes. Serve in bowls.

As an extra garnish, toss bread crumbs in melted butter until lightly coated and mix with grated cheese as a topping. Brown slightly under broiler for a beautiful finished look.

"Feels like a down home Prince Edward Island picnic... easy, time-saving recipes."　　　*Harrowsmith Country Life Magazine*

Three Pepper Veggie Toss

Chopped onion	1 med	1 med
Chopped garlic	1 clove	1 clove
Italian seasoning	1 tsp	5 ml
Olive oil	2 tbsp	30 ml
Water	1/4 cup	60 ml
Beef bouillion	2 tsp	10 ml
Cauliflower florets	1/2 cup	125 ml
Broccoli florets	1/2 cup	125 ml
Zucchini	2 sm	2 sm
Red pepper	1	1
Green pepper	1	1
Orange pepper	1	1
Balsamic vinaigrette	1/4 cup	60 ml
Spaghetti noodles, cooked	1/3 pkg	.33 pkg
Salt	to taste	to taste
Pepper	to taste	to taste
Parmesan cheese	1/2 cup	125 ml

In a large skillet, heat olive oil and cook and stir onion, garlic and Italian seasoning until tender. Add water, beef bouillion and veggies (cut peppers into thin, short strips). Cover and simmer about 10 minutes. Toss with hot pasta. Add vinaigrette, cheese, salt and pepper to taste.

See photo page 127.

Pepperonata

Olive oil	4 tbsp	60 ml
Finely sliced onion	1 lg	1 lg
Red pepper in strips	2	2
Green pepper in strips	2	2
Orange pepper in strips	2	2
Yellow pepper in strips	2	2
Crushed garlic	2 cloves	2 cloves
Chopped tomatoes	2 cans	2 cans
Chopped parsley	2 tbsp	30 ml

Heat the oil in a large skillet. Add the onion and sauté for 5 minutes, stirring until just beginning to colour. Add the bell peppers and garlic to the pan and cook a further 3-4 minutes.

Stir in the tomatoes and parsley and season with salt and pepper. Cover the skillet and cook the vegetables gently for about 30 minutes or until mixture is dry.

Red Pepper Barley Casserole

Butter	1/4 cup	60 ml
Chopped onion	1 lg	1 lg
Minced garlic	2 cloves	2 cloves
Barley	1 1/2 cups	375 ml
Beef stock	4 cups	1000 ml
Worcestershire sauce	2 tsp	10 ml
Bay leaf	1	1
Thyme	1 tsp	5 ml
Red pepper	1	1
Celery	2 stalks	2 stalks
Salt and pepper	to taste	to taste

Melt butter in large saucepan; cook onion and garlic until fragrant and softened. Stir in barley, stock, worcestershire sauce, bay leaf and thyme. Bring to a boil on medium heat. Simmer, covered for 35 minutes or until barley is tender. Discard bay leaf and season with salt and pepper. Stir in sliced/chopped red pepper and diagonally sliced celery.

Spoon into a 6 cup casserole. Cover and refrigerate up to 1 day. Bring to room temperature, about 1 hour before serving and bake at 400° for 25 minutes or until heated through. Serves 8.

Tasty Potato Slices

Peeled, sliced potatoes	4 cups	1000 ml
Honey mustard salad dressing	1/2 cup	125 ml
Salt	1/2 tsp	2 ml
Pepper	1/2 tsp	2 ml
Chives	1 tsp	5 ml

In a large bowl, combine all ingredients. Transfer to a greased 13 x 9 x 2 inch baking pan. Bake, uncovered at 350° for 50-55 minutes or until tender. Stir before serving. Serves 4.

See photo page 73.

Hint! Hot peppers will be hotter with warmer weather and less water.

Potato Carrot Kugel

Vegetable Oil	2 tbsp	30 ml
Thinly sliced onion	1 med	1 med
Sliced mushrooms	3 cups	750 ml
Dried thyme	1 1/2 tsp	7 ml
Baking potatoes	4 med	4 med
Carrots	2 lg	2 lg
Eggs	3	3
Salt	3/4 tsp	3 ml
Black pepper	1/2 tsp	2 ml
Shredded cheddar	1 cup	250 ml

In a large frying pan, heat oil over medium heat; cook onion, mushrooms and thyme, stirring occasionally for about 10 minutes until softened. Place in large bowl. Peel and grate potatoes and carrots. Add to onion mixture and toss to mix.

Whisk together eggs, salt and pepper. Add to potato mixture. Add cheese and toss to combine well.

Spoon into greased 11 x 7 inch (2 l) baking dish. Bake in top of 400° oven for one hour until golden and crispy. Makes 4 main course servings.

See photo page 73.

Margo's Swedish Potatoes

Potatoes	6 lg	6 lg
Light sour cream	3/4 cup	175 ml
Light cream cheese	4 oz	125 g
Onion salt	1 1/2 tsp	7 ml
Pepper	1 1/2 tsp	7 ml
Butter	3 1/2 tbsp	50 ml
Bread crumbs	3/4 cup	175 ml

Cook potatoes in salted boiling water until tender. Drain; mash until smooth. Add sour cream, room temperature cream cheese, onion salt, pepper and 2 tbsp of butter. Beat until fluffy with electric beater. Turn into a well buttered casserole.

Melt 1 1/2 tbsp butter, add bread crumbs and toss until moist. Cover potatoes with topping, bake at 350° for about 30 minutes.

Hint!   Be careful not to cross contaminate. Use separate cutting boards for produce, chicken and seafood.

French Scalloped Potatoes

Thinly sliced potatoes	2 1/2 lbs	1250 g
Butter	4 tbsp	60 ml
Salt and pepper	to taste	to taste
Shredded swiss cheese	1 1/2 cups	375 ml
Beef stock	1 cup	250 ml
Egg	1	1
Sour cream	1/2 cup	125 ml
Whipping cream	1/2 cup	125 ml

Preheat oven to 425°. Drop sliced potatoes into pan of cold water, bring to a boil and cook for 10-12 minutes. Drain potatoes and dry on large tea towel.

Arrange overlapping layers of potatoes in casserole, dotting each with a layer of butter, sprinkling with salt, pepper and cheese. Repeat layers ending with cheese (keep back 3 tbsp of cheese).

Bring beef stock almost to a boil. Pour over potatoes. Bake for 45 minutes, covering loosely with foil. When potatoes are tender, remove from oven.

For cream topping, beat egg into creams and 3 tbsp of cheese and spread over casserole. Return to oven until golden, about 5 minutes. Garnish with parsley.

PEI Potato Pie

Flour	2 cups	500 ml
Shortening	1 cup	250 ml
Salt	1 tsp	5 ml
Dried mixed herbs	1 tsp	5 ml
Water	3-4 tbsp	45-60 ml
Cottage cheese	1 lb	500 g
Mashed potatoes	2 cups	500 ml
Sour cream	1/2 cup	125 ml
Eggs	2	2
Salt	2 tsp	10 ml
Cayenne	1/8 tsp	.5 ml
Green onions	1/2 cup	125 ml
Grated cheddar cheese	1 cup	250 ml

Cut shortening into flour, salt and seasonings. Add cold water. Mix with fork and roll into a ball. Divide in half. Roll out crust for pie plate; refrigerate other half.

Beat cottage cheese, mashed potatoes and other ingredients until smooth. Spoon into pastry shell. Sprinkle with grated cheddar cheese. Bake at 350° for 50 minutes or until nicely browned. Can be partially cooked and finished prior to serving. May be served hot or cold!

See photo page 73.

Slow Cooked Potatoes

Potatoes	6 med	6 med
Shredded cheddar cheese	2 cups	500 ml
Cream of celery soup condensed	10 3/4 oz can	300 g can
Chopped onion	1 sm	1 sm
Butter, divided	7 tbsp	100 ml
Salt	1 tsp	5 ml
Pepper	1 tsp	5 ml
Sour cream	1 cup	250 ml
Seasoned croutons	2 cups	500 ml

Toss the peeled potatoes which have beeen cut into 1/4 inch thick strips and cheese; place in 5 quart slow cooker. Combine soup, onion, 4 tbsp butter, salt and pepper; pour over potato mixture.

Cover and cook on low for 8-10 hours or until potatoes are tender. Stir in sour cream. Toss croutons and remaining butter; sprinkle over potatoes. Makes 10-12 servings.

Three Potato, Four!

1. Potato Carrot Kugel, page 70
2. Hot Milk Potato Stuffing, page 144
3. Two Colour Baked Potatoes, page 79
4. Tasty Potato Slices, page 69
5. PEI Potato Pie, page 71

Flowers:

Bachelor's Buttons 'Polka Dot', Golden Chamomile.

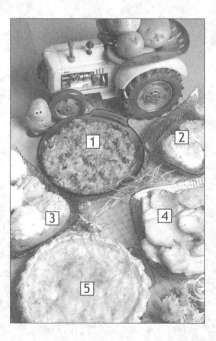

Eleanor's Mom's Potato Salad

Miracle whip	1 cup	250 ml
Prepared mustard	1 tsp	5 ml
Celery seed	1/2 tsp	2 ml
Salt	1/2 tsp	2 ml
Pepper	1/8 tsp	.5 ml
Cubed cooked potatoes	4 cups	1000 ml
Finely chopped hard boiled eggs	2	2
Chopped onions	1/2 cup	125 ml
Chopped celery slices	1/2 cup	125 ml
Chopped Gherkin pickles	1/2 cup	125 ml
Peas	1/4 cup	60 ml

Stir together Miracle Whip, mustard, celery seed, salt and pepper. Add remaining ingredients. Mix lightly. Chill covered for several hours before serving.

See photo on facing page.

Summer Supper

1. Blueberry Oat Treats, page 112
2. Beet Relish, page 16
3. Alice's Lime Cucumber Salad, page 46
4. Surprise Cole Slaw, page 30
5. Eleanor's Mom's Potato Salad, page 75

Flower arrangement:

German Statice, Globe Thistle, Ageratum, Pansies Celestial Blue.

Cheesy Potatoes

Sour cream	1 cup	250 ml
Milk	1/2 cup	125 ml
Minced chives	1 tbsp	15 ml
Italian seasoning	1 tsp	5 ml
Salt	1/2 tsp	2 ml
Pepper	1/4 tsp	1 ml
Sliced potatoes	6 med	6 med
Shredded old cheddar	1 cup	250 ml
Crushed Honeynut		
Cornflakes	1/2 cup	125 ml

In a large bowl, combine sour cream, milk, chives, and seasonings. Add potatoes which have been sliced 1/4 inch thick, and mix thoroughly. Spread in a 13 x 9 x 2 inch baking dish. Combine cheese and Honeynut Cornflakes (crushed); sprinkle over potatoes. Bake at 350° for 50-60 minutes or until potatoes are tender. Sprinkle with additional chives if desired. Makes 6-8 servings.

Cottage Potatoes

Chopped, crisp bacon	1/4 lb	125 g
Cubed potatoes	12 lg	12 lg
Cubed Velveeta	8 oz	250 g
Diced green pepper	1	1
Chopped onion	1	1
Bread	1 slice torn	1 slice torn
Fresh parsley	3 tbsp	45 ml
Salt	1/2 tsp	2 ml
Milk	1/2 cup	125 ml
Melted butter	1/2 cup	125 ml
Crushed cornflakes	1 cup	250 ml

Place the potatoes in a large saucepan and cover with water. Bring to a boil; reduce heat to medium. Cover and cook for 5-7 minutes or until tender; drain. In a bowl, combine the cheese, onion, green pepper, bacon, bread, 2 tbsp parsley and salt.

In a greased shallow 4 qt baking dish, layer a third of the potatoes and a third of cheese mixture. Repeat layers twice. Pour milk and butter over all: sprinkle with cornflake crumbs. Cover and bake at 350° for 45 minutes. Uncover; bake 10-15 minutes longer or until bubbly and top is golden. Sprinkle with remaining parsley.

Makes 12-14 servings.

See photo page 92.

Hint! For great flavoured potatoes, add 1-2 cloves of mashed garlic to the water when cooking.

Twice Baked New Potatoes

New potatoes	1 1/2 lbs	750 g
Oil	2-3 tbsp	30-45 ml
Shredded Monterey Jack	1 cup	250 ml
Sour cream	1/2 cup	125 ml
Cream cheese	3 oz	85 g
Minced onion	1/3 cup	75 ml
Basil	1 tsp	5 ml
Garlic	1 clove	1 clove
Salt and pepper	to taste	to taste
Crumbled, crisp bacon	1/2 lb	250 g

Pierce potatoes, rub with oil. Bake at 400° for 50 minutes or until tender. Cool to touch.

In a bowl, combine cheese, sour cream, cream cheese, seasonings. Cut potatoes in half, scoop out pulp. Add pulp to cheese mixture; mash, stir in bacon, stuff shells.

Broil 7-8 minutes.

Crunchy Curried Potato Salad

Potatoes (unpeeled)	5 med	5 med
Butter	1 tbsp	15 ml
Finely chopped onion	1 med	1 med
Curry	1 1/2 tsp	7 ml
Celery	4 stalks	4 stalks
Peeled, chopped apple	1 med	1 med
Mayonnaise	1 cup	250 ml
Lemon juice	1 tbsp	15 ml
Salt	1 tsp	5 ml
Pepper	1 tsp	5 ml

Boil potatoes until cooked but firm. Rinse with cold water. Sauté onion in butter, add curry, cook for 2 minutes.

Coarsely chop potatoes, celery and apple. Combine with curry mixture and mayonnaise, lemon juice and seasonings. Mix, cover, refrigerate 1 hour before serving.

Hint! To keep stored potatoes from sprouting, place an apple in your potato bin.

Bacon and Chive Potato Patties

Cooked bacon	3 strips	3 strips
Potatoes (peeled)	2 lg	2 lg
Fresh chives	1/4 cup	60 ml
Sour cream	1/2 cup	125 ml
Olive oil	1/3 cup	75 ml

Remove bacon fat from meat; chop bacon finely. Coarsely grate potatoes and press between layers of paper towel to remove as much moisture as possible.

Combine bacon, potatoes, chives and sour cream in a bowl. Mix well. Divide mixture into 8 portions and shape into equal sized patties.

Heat oil in a heavy pan, add patties a few at a time and cook until browned on both sides. Place patties in a single layer on oven pan; bake uncovered at 350° for about 20 minutes or until cooked through.

See photo page 37.

Sweet and Sour Potatoes

Diced potatoes	4 1/2 cups	1125 ml
Bacon	6 slices	6 slices
Finely chopped onion	1/3 cup	75 ml
Honey	1 1/2 tbsp	22 ml
Salt	3/4 tsp	3 ml
Water	1/2 cup	125 ml
Vinegar	1/4 cup	60 ml

Fry bacon in a skillet until crisp. Remove and crumble well. Drain all but 3 tbsp of grease. Using the 3 tbsp of bacon grease, cook potatoes over medium heat without turning for 20-25 minutes or until brown on the bottom. Turn with spatula, add onion and cook another 5 minutes. Stir in honey, salt and water.

Simmer until potatoes are tender, about 15 minutes. Remove from heat and add vinegar. Cover and let stand for 15 minutes. Remove cover, add bacon; stir. Reheat to serve hot.

See photo page 127.

Hint! *To stop water in pots from overflowing when cooking potatoes, dab 1 tbsp butter onto waxed paper and rub it along the inside of the pot about an inch below the lip. When heat causes the water to rise, the greased rim will repel it. This hint saves wear and tear on your stove top as well as clean up time.*

Two Colour Baked Potatoes

Potatoes	6 med	6 med
Sweet Potatoes	6 med	6 med
Sour cream	2/3 cup	150 ml
Blend cream	1/3 cup	75 ml
Shredded cheddar	3/4 cup	175 ml
Minced chives	4 tbsp	60 ml
Salt	1 1/2 tsp	7 ml

Pierce potatoes and sweet potatoes with a fork. Bake at 400° for 60-70 minutes or until tender. Set sweet potatoes aside. Cut a third off the top of each potato; scoop out pulp in a bowl, leaving skins intact. Place pulp in a bowl; mash with 1/3 cup sour cream, blend, cheese, 2 tbsp chives and 3/4 tsp salt. Set aside.

Cut off the top of each sweet potato; scoop out pulp, leaving skins intact. Mash pulp with remaining sour cream, chives and salt. Stuff mixture into half of each potato skin; spoon potato mixture into other half. Place on a baking sheet. Bake at 350° for 15-20 minutes or until heated through. Serves 12.

See photo page 73.

Island Potato Bannock

Flour	2 1/4 cups	560 ml
Wheat germ	1/3 cup	75 ml
Baking powder	4 tsp	20 ml
Baking soda	1/2 tsp	2 ml
Brown sugar	2 tbsp	30 ml
Salt	1/2 tsp	2 ml
Soft butter	1/4 cup	60 ml
Blend cream	1 cup	250 ml
Warm mashed potatoes	1/2 cup	125 ml
Italian seasoning	2 tsp	10 ml
Chives	2 tsp	10 ml

Blend all dry ingredients together. Cut in butter. Whip potatoes and blend cream together until no lumps remain. Make a well in center of dry ingredients; add blend mixture. Knead a few seconds over floured board. Pat into 6 to 7 inch circle. Bake at 425° for about 25 minutes or until lightly brown. Cut in wedges and serve warm.

See photo page 55.

Hint! When boiling potatoes for potato salad, add a little vinegar to the water. This will help them keep their shape while being diced.

Sweet Potato Layer Cake

Vegetable oil	1 1/2 cups	375 ml
Sugar	2 cups	500 ml
Separated eggs	4	4
Shredded sweet potato	1 1/2 cups	375 ml
Hot water	1/4 cup	60 ml
Vanilla extract	1 tsp	5 ml
Cake flour	2 1/2 cups	1125 ml
Baking powder	3 tsp	15 ml
Ground cinnamon	1 tsp	5 ml
Ground nutmeg	1 tsp	5 ml
Salt	1/4 tsp	1 ml
Chopped pecans	1 cup	250 ml

FROSTING:

Butter	1/2 cup	125 ml
Sugar	1 cup	250 ml
Evaporated milk	1 cup	250 ml
Beaten eggs	3	3
Flaked coconut	1 1/3 cups	325 ml
Chopped pecans	1 cup	250 ml
Vanilla extract	1 tsp	5 ml

In a mixing bowl, beat oil and sugar. Add egg yolks, one at a time, beating well after each addition. Add sweet potato, water and vanilla; mix well. In a small mixing bowl, beat egg whites until stiff; fold into sweet potato mixture. Combine flour, baking powder, cinnamon, nutmeg and salt; add to potato mixture. Stir in pecans. Pour into three greased 9 inch round cake pans. Bake at 350° for 22-27 minutes or until a cake tester inserted near the centre comes out clean. Cool for 10 minutes before removing to a wire rack.

In medium saucepan combine sugar, milk, butter and eggs. Cook over medium heat until mixture starts to bubble, stirring constantly. Stir in remaining ingredients. Cool slightly. Place one cake layer on a serving plate; spread with one third of the frosting. Repeat layers. Serves 10-12 guests.

See photo page 20.

Cranberry Sweet Potato Muffins

Flour	1 1/2 cups	375 ml
Sugar	1/2 cup	125 ml
Baking powder	2 tsp	10 ml
Salt	3/4 tsp	4 ml
Ground cinnamon	1/2 tsp	2 ml
Nutmeg	1/2 tsp	2 ml
Egg	1	1
Milk	1/2 cup	125 ml
Cold mashed sweet potatoes	1/2 cup	125 ml
Melted butter	1/4 cup	60 ml
Chopped cranberries	1 cup	250 ml
STREUSEL TOPPING:		
Brown sugar	1/4 cup	60 ml
Flour	1 tbsp	15 ml
Cinnamon	1 tsp	5 ml
Melted butter	1 tbsp	15 ml

In a bowl, combine flour, sugar, baking powder, salt, cinnamon and nutmeg. In a small bowl, combine egg, milk, sweet potatoes and butter; stir into dry ingredients just until moistened. Stir in cranberries. Fill greased or paper-lined muffin cups. Combine Streusel ingredients and put over batter. Bake at 375° for 18-22 minutes or until a toothpick inserted near center comes out clean. Cool in pan 10 minutes; remove to a wire rack. Makes 12 muffins.

See photo page 91.

Sweet Potato Banana Muffins

Flour	1 3/4 cups	425 ml
Brown sugar	1/2 cup	125 ml
Baking powder	2 tsp	10 ml
Cinnamon	1 tsp	5 ml
Salt	1/2 tsp	2 ml
Mashed Sweet potatoes	1 1/2 cups	375 ml
Mashed bananas	2/3 cup	150 ml
Melted margarine	1/4 cup	60 ml
Eggs	2	2
Milk	3/4 cup	175 ml

In a bowl, combine flour, sugar, baking powder, cinnamon and salt. In another bowl combine sweet potatoes, bananas, eggs, milk and melted margarine. Add this to the flour mixture, stir to blend. Bake at 400° for 20 minutes. Makes 24 muffins.

See photo page 91.

Sweet Potato Quick Bread

Flour	3 1/2 cups	875 ml
Baking soda	2 tsp	10 ml
Baking powder	1 tsp	5 ml
Ground cinnamon	1 tsp	5 ml
Ground nutmeg	1 tsp	5 ml
Salt	1/2 tsp	2 ml
Ground cloves	1/2 tsp	2 ml
Mashed sweet potatoes	2 cups	500 ml
Eggs	3	3
Vegetable oil	1 cup	250 ml
Sugar	3 cups	750 ml
Chopped pecans	1 cup	250 ml

GLAZE:

Icing sugar	1 1/2 cups	375 ml
Orange juice	4-5 tsp	20-25 ml
Grated orange peel	1 tsp	5 ml

In a large bowl, combine the first seven ingredients. In another bowl, whisk the sweet potatoes, eggs and oil. Add sugar; whisk until smooth. Stir into dry ingredients just until combined. Fold in pecans (batter will be thick). Transfer to two greased 9 x 5 x 3 inch loaf pans.

Bake at 350° for 65-70 minutes or until a wooden skewer inserted almost to the bottom of the pan comes out clean. Cool for 10 minutes before removing from pans to wire racks to cool completely. For glaze, combine the icing sugar, orange juice and orange peel until blended; drizzle over loaves.

See photo page 56.

Sweet Potato Salad

Sweet potatoes	3 lbs	1.5 kg
Chopped red pepper	1 cup	250 ml
Chopped onion	1/2 cup	125 ml
Mayonnaise	1 1/4 cups	310 ml
Salt	1 tsp	2 ml
Hot pepper sauce	1/8-1/4 tsp	.5-1 ml

In a large bowl combine sweet potatoes, pepper and onion. In small bowl blend mayonnaise, salt, pepper and hot sauce. Pour over sweet potato mixture, toss to coat. Cover and refrigerate 1 hour.

Sweet Potato Scones

Flour	1 1/3 cups	325 ml
Baking powder	4 tsp	20 ml
Salt	1 tsp	5 ml
Brown sugar	1 tbsp	15 ml
Mashed sweet potatoes	1/4 cup	60 ml
Milk	2/3 cup	150 ml
Melted butter	1/4 cup	60 ml

Preheat oven to 450°. Sift the flour, baking powder and salt into a bowl. Add the sugar and stir to mix. In a separate bowl, combine the sweet potatoes with the milk and melted butter. Mix well until evenly blended.

Stir the dry ingredients into the sweet potato mixture to make a dough. Turn on to a slightly floured surface and knead lightly, just to mix, for 1-2 minutes. Roll or pat out the dough to 1/2 inch in thickness. Stamp out rounds with a cutter.

Arrange the rounds on a greased baking sheet. Bake until puffed and lightly golden, about 15 minutes. Serve warm. Makes 12 scones.

See photo page 19.

Tasty Glazed Sweet Potatoes

Sweet potatoes	3 lbs	1.5 kg
Gravenstein apples	2 lbs	1 kg
Maple syrup	3/4 cup	175 ml
Apple cider	1/4 cup	60 ml
Butter	1/4 cup	60 ml
Salt	1/2 tsp	2 ml

Peel the sweet potatoes; core and peel apples. Cut the sweet potatoes and apples into 1/4 inch slices. Layer in a greased 13 x 9 x 2 inch baking dish.

In a saucepan, bring syrup, cider, butter and salt to a boil. Pour over sweet potatoes and apples. Cover and bake at 350° for 1 hour. Uncover and bake 10-15 minutes longer or until tender. Makes 8-10 servings.

Upside Down Sweet Potato Cake

Sliced pineapple	1 can (20oz)	1 can(625g)
Butter	1 tbsp	15 ml
Light brown sugar	1/4 cup	60 ml
Ground ginger	1 tsp	5 ml
Dried cranberries	1/4 cup	60 ml
Gingerbread cake mix	pkg 14 1/2oz	pkg 435 g
Peeled and grated sweet potatoes	1 1/2 cups	375 ml
Eggs	2	2

Preheat oven to 350°. Drain pineapple, reserving 1/2 cup plus 3 tbsp juice. Set aside 7 whole pineapple slices. Place butter in a 9 x 2 inch round cake pan in oven until butter is melted. In a small bowl, combine the light brown sugar, ginger and 3 tbsp pineapple juice. Pour mixture in the pan and tilt to evenly distribute. Place the whole pineapple ring in the center; arrange remaining slices around the center. Fill in spaces with dried cranberries. In a bowl, combine cake mix, eggs, sweet potatoes and 1/2 cup pineapple juice. Using a fork, stir vigourously for about 2 minutes, scraping sides until well mixed. Spread batter over pineapple in pan. Bake for 45 to 50 minutes or until a cake tester comes out clean. Cool for 5 minutes, then invert onto platter, replacing any fruit that remains in the pan. Serve warm.

See photo page 20.

Lorraine's Pumpkin Walnut Cake

Flour	3 cups	750 ml
Baking powder	2 tsp	10 ml
Baking soda	2 tsp	10 ml
Salt	1 tsp	5 ml
Ground cinnamon	3 1/2 tsp	17 ml
Eggs	4 lg	4 lg
Granulated sugar	2 cups	500 ml
Corn oil	1 1/2 cups	375 ml
Pumpkin	2 cups	500 ml
Chopped walnuts	1 cup	250 ml

Sift together and set aside first 5 ingredients. In a large bowl, with mixer at high speed, beat eggs until yolks and whites are well combined. Gradually add sugar, beating until thick and lemony in colour, beating constantly. Pour in oil. With mixer at low speed, now blend in dry ingredients and cooked, mashed pumpkin (alternating), beginning and ending with dry ingredients. Beat smooth, stir in walnuts. Turn into a 10 inch ungreased tube pan. Bake 1 hour and 10 minutes in a 350° oven until tester comes out clean. Cool completely in cake pan on wire rack. Sprinkle with icing sugar for finished effect.

Pumpkin Pie for Dr. Jim

Salt	1/8 tsp	.5 ml
Sugar	2/3 cup	150 ml
Cinnamon	1 tsp	5 ml
Nutmeg	1/4 tsp	1 ml
Ginger	1/2 tsp	2 ml
Cloves	1/8 tsp	.5 ml
Slightly beaten eggs	2	2
Milk	1 2/3 cups	400 ml
Pumpkin	1 1/2 cups	375 ml
Uncooked pie shell	1	1

Sift dry ingredients together and stir into eggs. Add milk and cooked, mashed pumpkin. Pour filling into pie shell. Bake at 450° for 10 minutes. Reduce heat to 325° and bake 35 minutes longer or until knife inserted in centre comes out clean. Cool.

Pumpkin Bread

White sugar	1 1/2 cups	375 ml
Vegetable oil	1/2 cup	125 ml
Eggs	2	2
Water	1/3 cup	75 ml
Flour	1 3/4 cups	425 ml
Cinnamon	1 1/2 tsp	7 ml
Nutmeg	1 tsp	5 ml
Baking soda	1 tsp	5 ml
Salt	1/2 tsp	2 ml
Mashed pumpkin	1 cup	250 ml
Chopped pecans	1/2 cup	125 ml
Raisins or choc. chips	1/2 cup	125 ml

In electric mixer bowl beat sugar, oil, eggs and water until combined. Sift into this mixture the flour, baking soda and spices. Mix until moistened. Stir in pumpkin, pecans and raisins (or chocolate chips). Spoon batter into 2 greased and floured one pound coffee cans or four 19oz bean cans.

Bake at 350° for 40 minutes or until wooden cake tester inserted in center comes out clean. Let cool in cans for 10 minutes before removing. Once cool, slice into rounds.

See photo page 56.

Pumpkin Cake Roll

Eggs	3	3
Sugar	1 cup	250 ml
Cooked pumpkin	2/3 cup	150 ml
Lemon juice	1 tsp	5 ml
Flour	3/4 cup	175 ml
Cinnamon	2 tsp	10 ml
Baking powder	1 tsp	5 ml
Salt	1/2 tsp	2 ml
Nutmeg	1/4 tsp	1 ml
Cloves	1/2 tsp	2 ml
Chopped pecans	1 cup	250 ml

CREAM CHEESE FILLING:

Cream cheese	2 pkg (3 oz)	2 pkg (85 g)
Icing sugar	1 cup	250 ml
Butter	1/4 cup	60 ml
Vanilla	1/2 tsp	2 ml

In mixing bowl beat eggs for 5 minutes. Gradually beat in sugar until thick and lemon coloured. Add lemon juice and pumpkin. Combine dry ingredients and fold into pumpkin mixture.

Grease a 15 x 10 x 1 inch baking sheet, line with waxed paper. Grease and flour the paper.

Spread batter on pan, sprinkle with pecans (optional). Bake at 375° for 15 minutes.

Immediately turn onto tea towel dusted with icing sugar. Peel off paper, roll cake up in a towel, starting with short end. Cool.

In bowl, mix filling ingredients; unroll cake and spread filling to within 1 inch of sides. Roll up again, cover and chill. Dust with icing sugar before serving.

Hint!   Butter should be melted on top of the stove rather than in the microwave in order to retain its rich flavour.

Honey Pumpkin Pie

Cooked, mashed pumpkin	2 cups	500 ml
Evaporated milk	1 cup	250 ml
Honey	3/4 cup	175 ml
Slightly beaten eggs	3	3
Flour	2 tbsp	10 ml
Cinnamon	1 tsp	5 ml
Ginger	1/2 tsp	2 ml
Vanilla	1/2 tsp	2 ml
Pumpkin pie spice	1 tsp	5 ml
Pastry crust	1 - 9"	1 - 22 cm

Combine all ingredients in large bowl and beat until well mixed. Pour into crust. Bake at 400° for 45 minutes or until knife comes out clean. Serve warm with whipped cream on the side.

Radish Cucumber Side Salad

Peeled, cubed cucumber	4 cups	1000 ml
Salt	sprinkle	sprinkle
Thinly sliced radishes	1/3 cup	75 ml
Thinly sliced green onions	1/4 cup	60 ml
Grated carrot	1/4 cup	60 ml

DRESSING:

Mayonnaise	1/2 cup	125 ml
Vinegar	4 tsp	20 ml
Granulated sugar	2 tsp	10 ml

Sprinkle cucumber with salt in dish. Let stand 60 minutes. Drain. Add rest of vegetables.

Mix dressing in a small bowl. Chill separately from veggies. Just before serving, mix two dishes together. Makes 4-6 servings.

See photo front cover.

87

Radish Dill Slaw

Grated radish	1 cup	250 ml
Chopped fresh dill	2 tbsp	30 ml
Thinly sliced celery	1 stalk	1 stalk
Shredded green cabbage	2 cups	500 ml
DRESSING:		
Wine vinegar	2 tbsp	30 ml
Vegetable oil	1 tbsp	15 ml
Granulated sugar	2 tsp	10 ml
Dijon mustard	2 tsp	10 ml
Salt	1/4 tsp	1 ml
Pepper	1/4 tsp	1 ml

Whisk together all dressing ingredients in a medium bowl. Toss dressing with vegetables and refrigerate. Serves 4.

Radish and Squash Sauté

Radish, quartered	2 cups	500 ml
Yellow summer squash	2	2
Chopped garlic	1 tbsp	15 ml
Butter	2 tbsp	30 ml
Fresh oregano	1 tbsp	15 ml

In a large frying pan, sauté radishes, squash, garlic in butter until crisp-tender. Stir occasionally. Add chopped fresh oregano and serve.

Spinach and Sausage Pie

Italian sausage	1 lb	500 g
Chopped onion	1 med	1 med
Eggs	6	6
Frozen chopped spinach	2 pkgs(10oz)	2 pkgs(300g)
Shredded mozzarella	2 cups	500 ml
Shredded cheddar	2 cups	500 ml
Ricotta cheese	1 cup	250 ml
Garlic powder	1/2 tsp	2 ml
Pepper	1/4 tsp	1 ml
10 inch pie pastry	2	2
Water	1 tbsp	15 ml

In a skillet, brown sausage and onion until the sausage is done and onion is tender. Separate 1 egg and set aside the yolk. In a mixing bowl, beat the remaining egg white and whole eggs. Stir in the sausage and onion, spinach (thawed and well drained), mozzarella, cheddar, ricotta, garlic powder and pepper. Line a 10 inch pie plate with bottom pastry. Add filling. Top with upper crust; seal and flute the edges. Cut slits in top crust. Combine water with reserved egg yolk; brush over top crust. Bake at 375° for 50 minutes or until golden brown. Let stand 10 minutes before serving. Serves 8.

Spinach and Feta Cheese Quiche

Frozen chopped spinach	1 pkg(10oz)	1 pkg(300g)
Eggs	4	4
Blend cream	1 cup	250 ml
Milk	1 cup	250 ml
Lemon juice	2 tbsp	30 ml
Chopped parsley	2 tbsp	30 ml
Crumbled feta cheese	1/4 lb	125 g
Parmesan cheese	3 tbsp	45 ml
Salt and pepper	dash	dash
'Garlic Plus' seasoning	to taste	to taste

Start with a baked and cooled pie shell. Defrost spinach and squeeze out as much moisture as possible. It should be fairly dry. Mix eggs, blend and milk. Add dash of salt and pepper, lemon juice, parsley and seasoning. Stir in spinach and feta cheese. Fill the crust and place the Parmesan on top. Bake at 375° for 30 to 40 minutes or until a knife inserted in center comes out clean. Cool for 10 minutes before serving.

Spinach Pasta Salad

Macaroni	1 pkg(7oz)	1 pkg(200g)
Fresh spinach	3 cups	750 ml
Fresh, sliced mushrooms	12 oz	375 g
Sliced red onion	1 med	1 med
Chopped bacon strips	6	6
Cornstarch	1 tbsp	15 ml
Sugar	1 tbsp	15 ml
Salt	1tsp	5 ml
Pepper	1/2 tsp	2 ml
Mayonnaise	3/4 cup	175 ml
Water	1 cup	250 ml
Cider vinegar	1/3 cup	75 ml

Cook macaroni according to package instructions; drain and cool. In a large bowl combine macaroni, spinach, mushrooms and onion; set aside. In a medium skillet, cook bacon until crisp. Remove with a slotted spoon to paper towels; discard all but 2 tbsp of drippings. In a small bowl, combine cornstarch, sugar, salt and pepper; whisk into drippings. Stir in mayonnaise; gradually mix in water and vinegar. Bring to a boil over medium heat, stirring constantly; boil for one minute. Pour over spinach mixture and toss well. Sprinkle with bacon bits. Serve immediately or refrigerate. Makes 12-16 servings.

Mid Morning Break

1. Cranberry S. Potato Muffins, page 81
2. S. Potato Banana Muffins , page 81
3. Honeydew Lemonade, page 149
4. Strawberry lemonade, page 152
5. Carrot and Pineapple Muffins, page 36
6. Zucchini Choc. Chip Muffins, page 106

Flowers:

Daisy 'Snow Lady'.

Spinach Stuffed Tomatoes

Tomatoes	6	6
Butter	2 tsp	10 ml
Finely chopped onion	1 sm	1 sm
Minced garlic	1 clove	1 clove
Frozen chopped spinach	1 pkg(12oz)	1 pkg(350g)
Milk	1/3 cup	75 ml
Salt and pepper	to taste	to taste

TOPPING:

Cubed bread	2 tbsp	30 ml
Parsley	2 tbsp	30 ml
Parmesan cheese	2 tsp	10 ml
Butter	2 tbsp	30 ml
Herb and Garlic seasoning	1 tsp	5 ml

Cut a slice from top of each tomato. Scoop out pulp to halfway down tomato and save for sauce or soup. In a skillet, melt butter. Stir in spinach, chopped onion, minced garlic, milk, salt and pepper. Spoon mixture into tomatoes and arrange on baking sheet.

Topping: Combine cubed bread, parsley, cheese and seasonings in melted butter; place over top of tomatoes. Bake at 400° for 20 minutes or until heated through. Makes 6 servings.

Company Dinner

1. Hidden Surprise Carrot Cake, page 35
2. Turnip and Apple Bake, page 100
3. Cottage Potatoes, page 76
4. Beets Russian, page 16
5. Broccoli and Cauliflower Bake, page23
6. Pork Chop with sauce

Flower arrangement:

Lace Flower 'Queen of Africa', Romance Verbena, Cosmos 'Seashells', Cosmos 'Sensation Mix'.

Honey Dressed Spinach Salad

Fresh spinach	10 oz	300 g
Iceberg lettuce	1 sm	1 sm
Sliced green onions	2	2
Chopped green pepper	3 tbsp	45 ml
Cucumber, quartered	1 med	1 med
Drained mandarin oranges	1 can	1 can
Sunflower seeds	1/2 cup	125 ml
Mayonnaise	3/4 cup	175 ml
Honey	2 tbsp	30 ml
Lemon juice	1 tbsp	15 ml

In a large bowl. combine the first seven ingredients. In a small bowl, stir mayonnaise, honey and lemon juice until smooth. Pour over the salad and toss to coat. Serve immediately. Serves 8 to 10.

Butternut Apple Crisp

Brown sugar	3/4 cup	175 ml
Lemon juice	2 tbsp	30 ml
Ground cinnamon	1 tsp	5 ml
Salt	1/2 tsp	2 ml
Butternut squash	3-4 cups	750-1000 ml
Apple pie filling	20 oz can	625 g can
Flour	1/3 cup	75 ml
Quick cooking oats	2/3 cup	150 ml
Butter	1/3 cup	75 ml
Cinnamon	1/2 tsp	2 ml

Combine 1/2 cup brown sugar, lemon juice, cinnamon, salt, squash (peeled, sliced and uncooked), and pie filling. Spoon into a 11 x 9 x 2 inch greased baking dish. Cover and bake at 375° for 30 minutes. Combine remaining ingredients until crumbly. Sprinkle over squash mixture. Bake, uncovered, about 45 minutes longer or until squash is tender. Serve warm. Makes 8 servings.

Hint!   To save time when preparing squash for cooking, prick the squash with a fork and warm it in the microwave using a low setting. Once it is warm, it can be sliced open much easier.

Hint!   Squash is ready to harvest when the rind is hard to pierce with your thumb nail.

Squash Casserole

Yellow squash	8 cups	2000 ml
Chopped onion	1/2 cup	125 ml
Shredded carrots	3/4 cup	175 ml
Butter	1/4 cup	60 ml
Condensed cream of mushroom soup	10 3/4 oz can	325 g can
Sour cream	1/2 cup	125 ml
Seasoned cubed bread	2 cups	500 ml

Cook squash in lightly salted boiling water for 3 to 4 minutes or until crisp-tender. In a skillet, sauté onion and carrots in butter until tender. Combine onion and carrots with soup, sour cream and 1 1/2 cups of the cubed bread. Add squash and mix lightly. Spoon into a lightly greased 12 x 8 x 2 inch baking dish or a 2 quart casserole. Sprinkle with the remaining bread cubes. Bake uncovered at 350° for 25 minutes or until heated through. Makes 8 to 10 servings.

Swiss Chard Sauté

Swiss chard	3 lb	1.5 kg
Virgin olive oil	3 tbsp	45 ml
Chopped garlic	1 tbsp	15 ml
Salt	to taste	to taste
Roasted garlic flakes	pinch	pinch
Pepper flakes	pinch	pinch

Fill sink with cold water and wash Swiss chard to remove any grit. Transfer to paper towels and allow to dry for a few minutes. Remove the thick part of each stem by cutting a V-shaped notch partway into the leaf. Split each leaf in half lengthwise by slicing down the center rib. Stack the halved leaves and cut them crosswise to get 4 to 6 inch pieces.

Heat the oil in a large skillet over medium-high heat for 1 minute. Working in batches, pile the Swiss chard into the pan, turning and tossing gently until the leaves begin to wilt and turn glossy. Add a new batch of leaves as the previous batch wilts and makes room for more.

When all the Swiss chard is wilted, sprinkle in the chopped garlic and a little salt and toss well. Lower the heat to medium low, cover and cook for 4 minutes. Remove the lid, raise the heat to high, add the roasted garlic and pepper flakes and continue to cook for 2 to 3 minutes so that much of the liquid evaporates; the leaves should be tender but not overly soft. Serve immediately.

Tomato Scallop

Diced ripe tomatoes	1 cup	250 ml
Crumbled bread	2 slices	2 slices
Melted butter	1 1/2 tbsp	22 ml
Grated onion	2 tbsp	30 ml
Salt	to taste	to taste
Pepper	to taste	to taste
Brown sugar	2 tbsp	30 ml

Mix tomatoes with onion, salt, pepper and brown sugar. Toss bread crumbs in melted butter. Put tomato mixture in a greased casserole dish. Top with buttered bread crumbs.

Bake at 350° until lightly browned.

Tomato Basil Squares

Chilled pizza crust	1 pkg(10oz)	1 pkg(300g)
Shredded mozzarella	2 cups	500 ml
Parmesan cheese	1/4 cup	60 ml
Fresh basil leaves	2 tbsp	30 ml
Dried basil leaves	2 tsp	10 ml
Mayonnaise	2/3 cup	150 ml
Minced garlic	1 clove	1 clove
Sliced plum tomatoes	4	4

Preheat oven to 375°. Roll pizza crust onto a 12 x 15 inch pan. Sprinkle crust with 1 cup mozzarella cheese. Using cheese grater, grate parmesan cheese. In bowl, combine remaining mozzarella cheese, parmesan cheese, basil and mayonnaise; mix well and add minced garlic.

Thinly slice tomatoes; arrange in a single layer over top of mozzarella cheese on crust. Spoon mozzarella cheese mixture over tomatoes; spread to cover evenly. Bake 15 to 20 minutes or until top is golden and bubbly. Serve warm. Cut with a pizza cutter.

See photo page 38.

Hint! Tomatoes can't be ripened off the vine until they begin to turn colour on the vine.

Tomato Broccoli Cups

Soft bread crumbs	1 1/2 cups	375 ml
Grated parmesan cheese	1 cup	250 ml
Chopped green onions	2	2
Tomatoes	6-8 med	6-8 med
Chopped broccoli	2 cups	500 ml
Shredded cheddar cheese	1 cup	250 ml
Mayonnaise	3/4 cup	175 ml
Salt	to taste	to taste
Pepper	to taste	to taste

Combine 1/2 cup of bread crumbs and 1/4 cup parmesan cheese; set aside. Cut a thin slice off the top of each tomato; scoop out pulp and place in a strainer to drain. Place tomatoes upside down on paper towels. Cook the broccoli until crisp-tender; drain. Chop tomato pulp and place in a large bowl. Add broccoli, cheddar cheese, mayonnaise, salt, pepper and remaining bread crumbs and parmesan; mix gently. Stuff tomatoes; place in a greased 11 x 7 x 2 inch baking dish. Sprinkle with reserved crumb mixture. Bake, uncovered at 375° for 30-40 minutes. Makes 6-8 servings.

Tomato Bread Casserole

Chopped green onions	2	2
Wedge cut tomatoes	8 med	8 med
Cubed, crustless bread	8 slices	8 slices
Melted butter	2/3 cup	150 ml
Salt	1 tsp	5 ml
Dried basil	1 tsp	5 ml
Dried thyme	1 tsp	5 ml
Garlic herb seasoning	2 tsp	10 ml
Grated parmesan cheese	3/4 cup	175 ml

Arrange tomatoes and chopped green onions in a greased 13 x 9 x 2 inch baking dish. Top with bread cubes. Combine butter, salt, basil, thyme and garlic herb seasoning; drizzle over bread, tomato and green onion layer. Sprinkle with cheese. Bake, uncovered at 350° for 30-35 minutes. Makes 8 to 10 servings.

Hint! Do not over-fertilize tomatoes as they will produce too much growth and not enough fruit.

Tomato Bacon Pie

Unbaked pastry shell	1 - 9"	1-22cm
1/4" sliced tomatoes	3 med	3 med
Crumbled bacon	10 strips	10 strips
Shredded cheddar	1 cup	250 ml
Mayonnaise	1 cup	250 ml
Parmesan cheese	2 tbsp	30 ml

Create pastry shell according to recipe found on page 71 *(PEI Potato Pie)*, bake and cool. Place tomatoes and parmesan cheese in the crust; sprinkle with bacon. In a bowl, combine the cheese and mayonnaise. Spoon over bacon in the center of the pie, leaving 1 inch around the edge. Bake at 350° for 30 to 40 minutes or until golden brown (cover edges with foil if necessary to prevent overbrowning). Makes 6 servings.

Tomato Cheese Pie

CRUST:

Bisquick	2 cups	500 ml
Cold water	1/2 cup	125 ml
Shredded cheddar	1 cup	250 ml

FILLING:

Shredded cheddar	1 cup	250 ml
Sliced tomatoes	4-5 med	4-5 med
Sliced green onions	4-5	4-5
Butter	2 tbsp	30 ml
Salt	pinch	pinch
Pepper	pinch	pinch
Oregano	pinch	pinch
Basil	pinch	pinch

Roll crust ingredients and place into pie plate. Bake at 375° until golden. Add shredded cheese to baked crust . Slice tomatoes and put them around outside edge of pie crust, making 2 or three rows leaving an open space in the centre.

Cut and sauté green onions in butter and place in centre of tomatoes. Sprinkle with salt, pepper, oregano and basil. Bake again for 10-15 minutes; protect edge of crust from overbrowning by covering with foil. Makes 4-6 servings.

See photo page 19.

Hint! To prevent blossom end rot, put down lime around tomatoes in the spring and keep them well watered once the fruit begins to form.

Tomato Salad Cups

Campari tomatoes	10 lg	10 lg
Crushed Ritz crackers	15	15
Chopped green onion	1	1
Chopped celery	1/4 cup	60 ml
Chopped broccoli	1/4 cup	60 ml
Chopped green pepper	1/4 cup	60 ml
Mayonnaise	1/2 cup	125 ml
Olives	5	5

Hollow out tomatoes, discard pulp, turn upside down on paper towels to drain.

Mix remaining ingredients, except olives, and stuff tomatoes. Top each tomato with an olive half.

See photo page 38.

Grambie's Vegetable Soup

Diced onion	1/2 med	.5 med
Diced carrots	1/2 cup	125 ml
Diced turnip	1/2 cup	125 ml
Diced celery	1/2 cup	125 ml
Diced potato	1/2 cup	125 ml
Butter	1/4 cup	60 ml
Salt	1/2 tsp	2 ml
Flour	1 tbsp	15 ml
Sugar	1 tsp	5 ml
Pepper	dash	dash
Toasted bread, crumbled	1 slice	1 slice
Poultry seasoning	1/2 tsp	2 ml
Seasoning salt	1/2 tsp	2 ml

Melt butter in stew pan and when hot add onions. Sauté carefully; do not burn. Add flour and when well mixed pour on gradually 2 cups boiling water. Add salt, sugar, pepper, bread and vegetables and enough boiling water to cover all, if needed.

Simmer until vegetables are tender. Keep in double boiler over hot water until ready to serve. Taste and add seasoning salt if necessary. You can also add 1 can of vegetable soup if you like, for colour.

Turnip and Apple Bake

Turnip	1 lg	1 lg
Butter	1 tbsp	15 ml
Peeled apples	1 1/2 cups	375 ml
Brown sugar	1/4 cup	60 ml
Cinnamon	pinch	pinch
TOPPING:		
Flour	1/3 cup	75 ml
Brown sugar	1/3 cup	75 ml
Butter	2 tbsp	30 ml

Peel, dice and cook turnip. Drain and mash adding butter. Slice apples and toss with sugar and cinnamon. Arrange alternate layers of mashed turnip and sliced apples in a greased casserole beginning and ending with turnip. Mix together until crumbly the three ingredients for the topping. Sprinkle over top of casserole. Bake at 350° for one hour. Serve hot. Makes 6 to 8 servings.

See photo page 92.

Mashed Turnips Extraordinaire

Turnip	1 sm	1 sm
Carrots	4 med	4 med
Brown sugar	2 tbsp	30 ml
Frozen orange juice concentrate	2 tbsp	30 ml
Butter	1 tbsp	15 ml
Nutmeg	pinch	pinch
Salt and pepper	to taste	to taste
Cinnamon	1/2 tsp	2 ml

Peel turnip and carrots. Cut into 3/4 inch chunks. Cook in separate pots; drain. Mash with a potato masher or in the food processor.

Combine turnip, carrots, sugar, orange juice, butter, nutmeg, cinnamon, salt and pepper to taste. Makes 8 servings

Hint!   Adding mashed carrots to turnip along with brown sugar and butter, mellows the turnip and adds flavour to the carrots.

100

Turnip Casserole

BOTTOM LAYER:

Turnip	1 med	1 med
Butter	2 tbsp	30 ml
Brown sugar	2 tbsp	30 ml
Parsley	sprinkle	sprinkle

WHITE SAUCE:

Butter	2 tbsp	30 ml
Flour	1 tbsp	15 ml
2% milk	1 cup	250 ml
Grated Monterey Jack	1/4 cup	60 ml

TOPPING:

Bread crumbs	1 1/2 cups	375 ml
Butter	1 tbsp	15 ml
Paprika	dash	dash

For bottom layer, cook turnip in salt water. Drain and mash with butter, parsley and brown sugar. Spread in dish.

To prepare white sauce, melt butter; add flour. Stir until creamy. Add milk. Boil until thickened. Add Monterey Jack cheese. Stir until cheese is dissolved. Spread over mashed turnip.

For the topping combine bread crumbs with butter. Rub together and sprinkle over white sauce. Sprinkle with paprika. Bake at 350° for 20-25 minutes.

Glazed Turnips

Peeled turnip	1 lb	500 g
Butter	1 oz	30 g
Castor sugar	2 tsp	10 ml

Peel turnip and cut into chunks. Cook in boiling (lightly salted), water until just tender. Drain off all but 2 to 3 tbsp of water. Add butter and Castor (very fine) sugar. Heat gently, shaking pan frequently until a slightly sticky brown glaze is formed. Spoon and mix glaze over turnips and serve.

Hint! Be sure to apply Boron or a fertilizer containing Boron to turnips to prevent brown watery centers.

Melon Blueberry Treat

Watermelon cubes	2 cups	500 ml
Cantaloupe	1/2	.5
Honeydew melon	1/2	.5
Blueberries	1 cup	250 ml
Honey	2 tbsp	30 ml
Lemon juice	2 tbsp	30 ml

Cut cantaloupe and honeydew melon into cubes or balls. In bowl, combine cantaloupe, honeydew, watermelon and blueberries.

In small dish, combine honey and lemon juice; stir until mixed. Pour over melons; toss to mix. Cover and refrigerate until serving time. Makes 6 servings.

Zucchini Carrot Muffins

Shredded carrot	2 cups	500 ml
Shredded zucchini	1 cup	250 ml
Peeled, shredded apples	1 cup	250 ml
Grated orange peel	2 tsp	10 ml
Flour	2 cups	500 ml
Sugar	1 1/4 cups	300 ml
Ground cinnamon	1 tsp	5 ml
Baking soda	2 tsp	10 ml
Salt	1/2 tsp	2 ml
Lightly beaten eggs	3	3
Vegetable oil	3/4 cup	175 ml
Vanilla extract	1 tsp	5 ml

Gently toss together carrot, zucchini, apple and orange peel; set aside. In a large bowl, combine flour, sugar, cinnamon, baking soda and salt. Separately, combine eggs, oil and vanilla; stir into dry ingredients just until moistened (batter will be thick). Fold in carrot mixture. Fill greased or paper lined muffin cups two-thirds full. Bake at 375° for 20-22 minutes or until muffins test done. Cool in pan 10 minutes before removing to a wire rack. Makes 18 standard sized muffins.

Hint! A watermelon is ripe when the spot resting on the ground is yellow or if the tendril closest to the melon has dried up.

Zucchini Meatball Stew

Lightly beaten egg	1	1
Dry bread crumbs	1/2 cup	125 ml
Barbecue sauce	1/4 cup	60 ml
Mustard	1 tbsp	15 ml
Salt	1/2 tsp	2 ml
Pepper	1/2 tsp	2 ml
Sliced green onion	2	2
Ground beef	1 lb	500 g

SAUCE:

Chopped onion	1 cup	250 ml
Minced garlic	2 cloves	2 cloves
Vegetable oil	1 tbsp	15 ml
Flour	2 tbsp	30 ml
Beef broth	1 1/2 cups	375 ml
Diced tomatoes	1 can(14oz)	1 can(420g)
Tomato paste	2 tbsp	30 ml
Bay leaf	1	1
Dried thyme	3/4 tsp	3 ml
Salt	1/2 tsp	2 ml
Sliced carrots	1 1/2 cups	375 ml
Chopped zucchini	1 1/2 cups	375 ml
Chopped green pepper	1 cup	250 ml
Minced fresh parsley	1 tbsp	15 ml
Cooked rotini pasta	2 cups	500 ml

Combine the first 7 ingredients; add beef and mix well. Shape into 1 inch balls. Cook meatballs on broiler pan in oven; set aside.

In large saucepan oven, sauté onion and garlic in oil until onion is tender. Blend in flour. Gradually add broth, stirring constantly; bring to a boil. Cook and stir 1 to 2 minutes or until thickened. Add tomatoes, paste and seasonings; mix well. Add meatballs and carrots; bring to a boil. Reduce heat; cover and simmer 30 minutes. Add zucchini and peppers; bring to a boil. Reduce heat; cover and simmer 10 - 15 minutes or until vegetables are tender. Add parsley and pasta. heat through. Remove bay leaf. Makes 6-8 servings.

See photo page 55.

Hint! Do not leave large zucchini on the plant as they will prevent new ones from forming.

Zucchini Chocolate Cake

Flour	2 cups	500 ml
Baking powder	1 tsp	5 ml
Baking soda	1 tsp	5 ml
Cinnamon	1 tsp	5 ml
Nutmeg	1/2 tsp	2 ml
Salt	1/2 tsp	2 ml
Cocoa	1/4 cup	60 ml
Eggs	3	3
Sugar	2 cups	500 ml
Oil	1/2 cup	125 ml
Buttermilk	3/4 cup	175 ml
Shredded zucchini	2 cups	500 ml
Vanilla	1 tsp	5 ml
Pecans	1 cup	250 ml
Grated orange peel	1 tsp	5 ml

Stir together the first seven ingredients; set aside. In a large bowl, beat eggs until very light. Gradually beat in sugar until mixture is fluffy and pale ivory. Slowly beat in oil. Stir in flour mixture one third at a time, alternating with buttermilk and zucchini. Blend lightly but thoroughly. Stir in nuts, vanilla and peel.

Put in greased layer pans or a 13 x 9 inch pan. Bake at 350° for 40-45 minutes if cooking in layer pans; 10 to 15 minutes longer if using a 13 x 9 pan.

Salmon Zucchini Cakes

Butter	1 tbsp	15 ml
Diced onion	1/2 cup	125 ml
Salmon (drained)	1 can(6oz)	1 can(170g)
Shredded zucchini	1 cup	250 ml
Lightly beaten eggs	2	2
Fresh parsley	1/3 cup	75 ml
Lemon juice	1 tsp	5 ml
Salt	1/2 tsp	2 ml
Pepper	1/8 tsp	.5 ml
Bread crumbs	1 cup	250 ml
Cooking oil	2 tbsp	30 ml

In a small saucepan, melt butter. Cook the onion until tender, but not brown. Remove from the heat. Add cooked onion to salmon, zucchini, eggs, parsley, lemon juice, seasonings and 1/2 cup bread crumbs. Stir until well combined. Shape into six 1/2 inch thick patties; coat with remaining bread crumbs. In a medium skillet, heat oil and cook the patties 3 minutes on each side or until golden brown. Makes 3 servings.

Zucchini Carrot Cake

Eggs	4	4
Sugar	2 cups	500 ml
Vegetable oil	1 1/3 cups	325 ml
Flour	2 1/2 cups	625 ml
Baking soda	2 tsp	10 ml
Baking powder	2 tsp	10 ml
Ground cinnamon	2 tsp	10 ml
Ground cloves	1 tsp	5 ml
Ground allspice	1 tsp	5 ml
Ground ginger	1 tsp	5 ml
Salt	1 tsp	5 ml
Shredded carrots	2 cups	500 ml
Shredded zucchini	2 cups	500 ml

FROSTING:

Cream cheese	1 pkg(3oz)	1 pkg(90g)
Butter	1/3 cup	75 ml
Icing sugar	3 1/2 cups	875 ml
Orange juice concentrate	2 tsp	10 ml
Grated orange peel	1 tsp	5 ml

In a large mixing bowl, beat eggs and sugar until frothy. Gradually beat in oil. Combine dry ingredients; add to batter. Beat 4 minutes. Stir in carrots, zucchini and nuts. Pour into three greased 9 inch baking pans. Bake at 350° for about 35 minutes or until top springs back when lightly touched. Cool 5 minutes before removing from pans. Cool thoroughly on a wire rack.

For frosting, beat cream cheese and butter in a large mixing bowl until smooth. Add sugar, orange juice concentrate and peel. Continue beating until creamy. Spread between the layers and over the top and side of the cake. Makes 12-14 servings.

Hint! Add grated zucchini or carrots to your spaghetti sauce or meatloaf; this adds plenty of extra nutrients to your meal.

Zucchini Dipsticks

Melted margarine	1/4 cup	60 ml
Unpeeled zucchini	4-5 med	4-5 med
Italian bread crumbs	1/2 cup	125 ml
Grated parmesan	1/2 cup	125 ml
Garlic powder	1/2 tsp	2 ml
Salt	1/2 tsp	2 ml
Pepper	1/4 tsp	1 ml
Egg	1	1

Prepare zucchini by cutting into 3 inch sticks; set aside.

Brush about half of the margarine over a large baking sheet; set aside. In a large plastic resealable bag, toss together bread crumbs, cheese, garlic powder, salt and pepper. Beat an egg in a shallow bowl or pie plate.

Dip zucchini sticks, one or two at a time, into the beaten egg . Let excess egg drip off and then drop sticks into bag of breadcrumb mixture. Shake to coat. Remove coated zucchini from bag and place on baking sheet. Drizzle remaining margarine evenly over breaded zucchini sticks. Bake at 425° for 12 to 15 minutes, turning once half way through baking time. Serve with flavoured mayonnaise or your favourite dipping sauce. Serves 4 to 6.

Zucchini Chocolate Chip Muffins

Flour	1 1/2 cups	375 ml
Sugar	3/4 cup	175 ml
Baking soda	1 tbsp	15 ml
Cinnamon	1 tsp	5 ml
Salt	1/2 tsp	2 ml
Egg	1	1
Vegetable oil	1/2 cup	125 ml
Milk	1/4 cup	60 ml
Vanilla	1 tsp	5 ml
Shredded zucchini	1 cup	250 ml
Chocolate chips	3/4 cup	175 ml

Combine flour, sugar, baking soda, cinnamon and salt. In a separate bowl, combine oil, egg, milk, and vanilla; mix well. Stir into dry ingredients. Fold in zucchini and chocolate chips. Fill muffin cups two-thirds full. Bake at 350° for 20-25 minutes.

See photo page 91.

Stuffed Zucchini Boats

Ground beef	1 lb	500 g
Chopped onion	1 lg	1 lg
Bread crumbs	1 1/2 cups	375 ml
Chopped spinach	1 1/2 cups	375 ml
Minced fresh parsley	1/2 cup	125 ml
Tomato sauce	1/2 cup	125 ml
Shredded parmesan	1/4 cup	60 ml
Beaten egg	1	1
Salt	1 tsp	5 ml
Dried thyme	1/2 tsp	2 ml
Zucchini	6 med	6 med
Water	1 cup	250 ml

In a large skillet, cook beef and onion over medium heat until meat is no longer pink; drain. Stir in bread crumbs, spinach, parsley, tomato sauce, parmesan cheese, egg, salt and thyme; set aside.

Cut each zucchini in half lengthwise. Scoop out seeds, leaving 1/4 inch shells. Spoon about 6 tbsp beef mixture into each zucchini half. Place in two ungreased 13 x 9 x 2 inch baking dishes. Pour 1/2 cup water into each dish. Cover and bake at 350° for 30 minutes. Uncover; bake 10 minutes longer or until zucchini is tender. Makes 6 servings.

Dressed Up Blackberries

Fresh blackberries	2 1/2 cups	1250 ml
Sugar	1/4 cup	60 ml
Frozen orange juice	1 tbsp	15 ml
Grated orange rind	1 rind	1 rind
Vanilla yogurt	3/4 cup	175 ml

To prepare orange sauce, combine sugar, orange juice and grated rind then stir in yogurt; set aside.

Wash blackberries. Remove any stems. Spoon sauce into individual dessert dishes and top with blackberries. Another option is to alternate layers of sauce and berries into a stemmed glass. Makes 4 servings

Black and Blue Cobbler

Flour	1 cup	250 ml
Sugar	1 1/2 cups	375 ml
Baking powder	1 tsp	5 ml
Salt	1/4 tsp	1 ml
Ground cinnamon	1 tsp	5 ml
Beaten eggs	2	2
Milk	2 tbsp	30 ml
Vegetable oil	2 tbsp	30 ml
Fresh blackberries	2 cups	500 ml
Fresh blueberries	2 cups	500 ml
Water	3/4 cup	175 ml
Grated orange rind	1 tsp	5 ml

In a bowl, combine flour, 3/4 cup of sugar, baking powder, salt and cinnamon. Combine eggs, milk and oil; stir into dry ingredients just until moistened. Spread the batter evenly onto the bottom of a greased 5 quart slow cooker. In a saucepan, combine berries, water, orange rind and remaining sugar; bring to a boil. Remove from the heat; immediately pour over the batter. Cover and cook on high for 2 to 2 1/2 hours or until a toothpick inserted in the batter comes out clean. Turn off cooker and let stand 30 minutes before serving. Add whipped cream if desired. Makes 6 servings.

Simply Strawberry

1. Very Berry Choc. Shortcake, page 121
2. Cheesecake Dip Strawberries, page 123
3. Double Dipped Strawberries, page 120
4. Strawberry Pie, page 121

Flower arrangement:

Impatiens 'Tempo Scarlet', Zinnia 'Pulcino Mix'.

Cinnamon Chocolate Fruit Tart

Chocolate graham crackers	15	15
Sugar	2 tbsp	30 ml
Melted butter	1/2 cup	125 ml
Semi-sweet chocolate chips	12 oz	375 g
Blend cream	2/3 cup	150 ml
Ground cinnamon	1/2 tsp	2 ml
Blackberries	1 1/4 cups	310 ml
Raspberries	1 1/4 cups	310 ml

In food processor, pulse crackers and sugar for 2 minutes, add 1/4 cup melted butter. Press mixture into greased 9 inch tart pan with removable bottom. Freeze for 20 minutes.

In bowl, combine chocolate chips and remaining melted butter. In saucepan, boil blend cream and cinnamon. Pour over chocolate. Let sit one minute; stir. Spread on crust.

Top with blackberries and raspberries. Lightly dust with icing sugar for effect.

See photo page 20.

Young at Heart

1. Watermelon Whale
2. Watermelon Peacock
3. Watermelon Cookies, page 153
4. Show Off melon Treat, page 32

Flowers:

Sunflower 'Junior', Peach Passion Sunflower, Rudbeckia 'Indian Summer', Lace Flower.

Peach Blueberry Crisp

Sliced peaches	2 cans	2 cans
Blueberries	2 cups	500 ml
Brown sugar	1/3 cup	75 ml
Flour	2 tbsp	30 ml
Cinnamon	2 tsp	10 ml
TOPPING:		
Flour	1/3 cup	75 ml
Quick rolled oats	2/3 cup	150 ml
Cinnamon	1 tsp	5 ml
Brown sugar	1 1/4 cup	310 ml
Butter	1/3 cup	75 ml

In an eight cup baking dish combine peaches and blueberries. In small bowl, combine sugar, flour and cinnamon; add to fruit and toss to mix.

Topping: Combine flour, rolled oats, sugar and cinnamon; with pastry blender, cut in butter until crumbly. Sprinkle over top of fruit mixture. Bake at 350° for 25 minutes or microwave on High for 10 minutes or until mixture is bubbling and fruit is barely tender. Serve warm or cold. Makes 8 servings.

Blueberry Oat Treats

Cinnamon	1 tsp	5 ml
Flour	1 1/2 cups	375 ml
Quick cooking oats	1 1/2 cups	375 ml
Sugar	1 1/2 cups	375 ml
Baking soda	1/2 tsp	2 ml
Cold butter	3/4 cup	175 ml
Blueberries	2 cups	500 ml
Cornstarch	2 tbsp	30 ml
Lemon juice	2 tbsp	30 ml

In a bowl, combine cinnamon, flour, oats, 1 cup sugar and baking soda. Cut in butter until mixture resembles coarse crumbs. Reserve 2 cups for topping. Press remaining crumb mixture into a greased 11 x 9 x 2 inch baking pan; set aside. In a saucepan, combine blueberries, cornstarch, lemon juice and remaining sugar. Bring to a boil; boil for 2 minutes, stirring constantly. Spread evenly over the crust. Sprinkle with the reserved crumb mixture. Bake at 375° for 25 minutes or until lightly browned. Cool before cutting. Makes 2 1/2 to 3 dozen.

See photo page 74.

Lemon Blueberry Scones

Flour	4 cups	1000 ml
Sugar	6 tbsp	90 ml
Baking Powder	4 1/2 tsp	22 ml
Salt	1/2 tsp	2 ml
Cold butter	1/2 cup	125 ml
Eggs	2	2
Milk	3/4 cup	175 ml
Blueberries	1 1/2 cups	375 ml
Grated lemon rind	2 tsp	10 ml

In a bowl combine the flour, sugar, baking powder, grated lemon rind and salt; cut in butter until mixture resembles coarse crumbs. In a bowl, whisk eggs and 3/4 cup milk; add to dry ingredients just until moistened. Turn onto a lightly floured surface; gently knead in the blueberries (if blueberries are frozen, do not thaw before adding).

Divide the dough in half. Pat each portion into an 8 inch circle; cut each into eight wedges. Place on greased baking sheets. Brush with additional remaining milk. Bake at 375° for 15-20 minutes or until tops are golden brown. Serve warm. Makes 16 scones.

See photo page 56.

French Toast Bake

Day old French bread	12 slices	12 slices
Eggs	5	5
Milk	2 1/2 cups	625 ml
Brown sugar	1 cup	250 ml
Vanilla extract	1 tsp	5 ml
Ground nutmeg	1/2 tsp	2 ml
Cinnamon	1 tsp	5 ml
Melted butter	1/4 cup	60 ml
Fresh or frozen blueberries	2 cups	500 ml

Arrange 1 inch thick slices of bread in a greased 13 x 9 x 2 inch baking dish. In a bowl, combine the eggs, milk, 3/4 cup brown sugar, vanilla, nutmeg and cinnamon; pour over bread. Cover and refrigerate for 8 hours or overnight.

Remove from the refrigerator 30 minutes before baking. Combine butter and remaining sugar; drizzle over the top. Bake, uncovered at 400° for 25 minutes. Sprinkle with blueberries. Bake 10 minutes longer or until a knife inserted near the center comes out clean.

See photo page 145.

113

Blueberry Bundt Cake

Egg whites	7	7
Sugar	1 3/4 cups	425 ml
Egg yolks	4	4
Oil	1 cup	250 ml
Vanilla	3 tsp	15 ml
Juice and rind of lemon	1	1
Flour	2 1/4 cups	500 ml
Baking powder	2 tsp	10 ml
Blueberries	1 cup	250 ml

Beat egg whites until stiff while gradually adding sugar. In a separate bowl, beat egg yolks, oil, vanilla and lemon juice and rind together then gradually fold them into the egg white mixture.

Sift flour and baking powder together and fold into mixture. Add blueberries to mixture. Put in a greased heavy cast iron casserole or bundt pan and bake in oven at 325° for one hour.

Chocolate Topped Fruit Cups

Sliced strawberries	1 cup	250 ml
Pineapple chunks	1 cup	250 ml
Fresh blueberries	1 cup	250 ml
Sliced apples	2 med	2 med
Peeled and sliced kiwi	3	3
Sliced banana	1	1
RICH CHOCOLATE SAUCE:	1 cup	250 ml
Butter	4 1oz squares	4 30g squares
Unsweetened chocolate	3 cups	750 ml
Sugar	1 cup	250 ml
Baking cocoa	2 cups	500 ml
Whipping cream	2 tsp	10 ml

Mix all fruit together; serve in individual cups or large stemmed glasses. Generously cover fruit with rich chocolate sauce.

To prepare sauce, melt butter and chocolate in a heavy saucepan over low heat. Stir in the sugar and cocoa until smooth. Gradually add cream; mix well. Cook for 10 minutes or until sugar is dissolved, stirring frequently. Remove from the heat; stir in vanilla.

See photo front cover.

Hint! Leftover chocolate sauce can be stored in the refrigerator and brought back to life by a quick zap in the microwave.

Kiwi Strawberry Dessert

Peeled and sliced kiwi	3	3
Sliced strawberries	2 cups	500 ml
Caramel ice cream topping	2 tbsp	30 ml
Orange juice	1 tbsp	15 ml
Toasted almonds	3 tbsp	45 ml

Place fruit in bowl. Combine caramel topping and juice, pour over fruit and top with almonds.

White Chocolate Fruit Tart

Butter	3/4 cup	175 ml
Icing sugar	1/2 cup	125 ml
Flour	1 1/2 cups	375 ml
Melted vanilla baking chips	1 pkg (10oz)	1 pk (300g)
Whipping cream	1/4 cup	60 ml
Cream cheese	8oz	250 g
Sliced strawberries	2 cups	500 ml
Sliced kiwi	4	4
Blueberries	1 cup	250 ml
Drained mandarin oranges (save juice)	1 can	1 can

GLAZE:		
Sugar	3 tbsp	45 ml
Cornstarch	2 tsp	10 ml
Lemon juice	1/2 tsp	2 ml

Cream butter and sugar. Gradually add flour, mix well. Press into greased 11" tart pan or 12" pizza pan. Bake at 300° for 25-30 minutes. Let cool.

In bowl, beat melted chips and cream, add cream cheese and beat until smooth. Spread over crust. Chill for 30 minutes. Arrange fruit over filling.

In saucepan, combine glaze ingredients and juice from can of mandarin oranges; bring to a boil. Boil for 2 minutes, until thickened, stirring constantly. Cool, brush over fruit.

Chill one hour before serving, store in fridge.

See photo front cover.

115

Raspberry Orange Swirls

Sugar	2/3 cup	150 ml
Cornstarch	2 tbsp	30 ml
Ground cinnamon	1/4 tsp	1 ml
Ground nutmeg	1/8 tsp	.5 ml
Salt	1/8 tsp	.5 ml
Water	1 cup	250 ml
Fresh raspberries	3 cups	750 ml

SWIRLS:

Flour	1 cup	250 ml
Baking powder	2 tsp	10 ml
Salt	1/2 tsp	2 ml
Shortening	3 tbsp	45 ml
Slightly beaten egg	1	1
Blend cream	2 tbsp	30 ml
Brown sugar	1/4 cup	60 ml
Melted butter	2 tbsp	30 ml
Grated orange peel	1 tsp	5 ml

In a saucepan, combine sugar, cornstarch, cinnamon, nutmeg and salt. Gradually add water; bring to a boil. Reduce heat to medium; cook and stir until the sauce thickens, about 5 minutes. Place berries in an ungreased 1 1/2 quart shallow baking dish; pour hot sauce over top. Bake at 400° for 10 minutes; remove from the oven and set aside.

For swirls, combine dry ingredients in a bowl; cut in shortening until crumbly. Combine egg and blend cream; stir into dry ingredients to form a stiff dough. Shape into a ball; place on a lightly floured surface. Roll into a 12 inch x 6 inch rectangle. Combine sugar, butter and orange peel; spread over dough. Roll up, jelly roll style, starting at a long side. Cut into slices; pat each slice to flatten slightly. Place on top of berry mixture.

Bake at 400° for 15 minutes or until swirls are golden. Garnish servings with cream and raspberries if desired. Makes 10 servings.

See photo page 37.

Raspberry Cheesecake

Chocolate wafer crumbs	1 1/3 cups	325 ml
Melted butter	1/3 cup	75 ml

RASPBERRY SAUCE:

Raspberries	2 1/2 cups	625 ml
Sugar	2/3 cup	150 ml
Cornstarch	2 tbsp	30 ml
Lemon juice	2 tsp	10 ml

FILLING/TOPPING:

Cream cheese	3 pkg(8oz)	3 pkg(250g)
Sugar	1/2 cup	125 ml
Flour	2 tbsp	30 ml
Vanilla extract	1 tsp	5 ml
Egg whites	2	2
Whipping cream	1 cup	250 ml
Orange juice	2-3 tbsp	30-45 ml
Raspberries	1 1/2 cups	375 ml

Combine the first two ingredients; press into bottom and 1 1/2" up sides of a greased 9 inch spring form pan. Chill one hour or until firm.

Puree raspberries in a blender or food processor. Press through a sieve; discard seeds. Add water if necessary to measure one cup. In a saucepan, combine sugar and cornstarch. Stir in raspberry juice; bring to a boil. Boil 2 minutes, stirring constantly. Remove from heat; stir in lemon juice and set aside.

In a mixing bowl, beat cream cheese, sugar, flour and vanilla until fluffy. Add egg whites; beat on low just until blended. Stir in cream. Pour half into crust. Top with 3/4 cup raspberry sauce (cover and refrigerate remaining sauce). Carefully spoon remaining filling over sauce.

Bake at 375° for 35-40 minutes or until center is nearly set. Remove from oven; immediately run a knife around pan to loosen crust. Cool on wire rack for 1 hour. Refrigerate overnight. Add orange juice to chilled raspberry sauce; gently fold in raspberries. Spoon over the cheesecake. Makes 12-16 servings.

Rhubarb Peach Pie

Sliced peaches	8 1/2 oz can	275 ml can
Chopped rhubarb	2 cups	500 ml
Sugar	1 cup	250 ml
Flaked coconut	1/4 cup	60 ml
Quick cooking tapioca	3 tbsp	45 ml
Almond extract	1 tsp	5 ml
Pie crust	2 - 9"	2 - 22cm
Butter	1 tbsp	15 ml

Drain peaches, reserving syrup; chop the peaches. Place peaches and syrup in a bowl; add rhubarb, sugar, coconut, tapioca and vanilla. Line a 9 inch pie plate with the bottom pastry.

Add filling; dot with butter. Top with remaining pastry; flute edges. If using a full top crust, cut slits in it. Bake at 350° for 1 hour or until crust is golden brown and filling is bubbly. Makes 6 to 8 servings.

Rhubarb Cereal Crisp

Rhubarb	4 cups	1000 ml
Flour	1 1/4 cups	310 ml
Sugar	1/4 cup	60 ml
Strawberry jam	1/2 cup	125 ml
Honey almond granola cereal	1 1/2 cups	375 ml
Brown sugar	1/2 cup	125 ml
Pecans	1/2 cup	125 ml
Ground cinnamon	1/2 tsp	2 ml
Cold butter	1/2 cup	125 ml

In a bowl, combine the rhubarb, 1/4 cup flour and sugar; stir in jam and set aside. In another bowl, combine the granola, brown sugar, pecans, cinnamon and remaining flour. Cut in butter until the mixture resembles coarse crumbs.

Press 2 cups of the granola mixture into a greased 8 inch square baking dish; spread rhubarb mixture over the crust. Sprinkle with remaining granola mixture. Bake at 375° for 30-40 minutes or until filling is bubbly and topping is golden brown. Serve warm with ice cream if desired. Makes 9 servings.

Streusel Topped Rhubarb Muffins

Brown sugar	1 1/4 cups	310 ml
Salad oil	1/2 cup	125 ml
Egg	1	1
Vanilla	2 tsp	10 ml
Buttermilk	1 cup	250 ml
Diced rhubarb	1 1/2 cups	375 ml
Chopped pecans	1/2 cup	125 ml
Flour	2 1/2 cups	625 ml
Baking powder	1 tsp	5 ml
Baking soda	1 tsp	5 ml
Salt	1/2 tsp	2 ml

TOPPING:

Butter	1 tbsp	15 ml
Sugar	1/3 cup	75 ml
Cinnamon	1 tsp	5 ml

Combine sugar, oil, egg, vanilla and buttermilk. Beat well. Stir in rhubarb and pecans. In another bowl mix flour, baking soda, baking powder and salt; blend throughly. Stir dry ingredients into wet; blend well. Spoon into large muffin papers in muffin tin.

Scatter cinnamon topping over tops and press lightly into batter. Bake 20-25 minutes in a 400° oven.

Rhubarb Pinwheels

Flour	2 cups	500 ml
Sugar	2 tbsp	30 ml
Salt	1 tsp	5 ml
Baking powder	4 tsp	20 ml
Cream of tartar	1/2 tsp	2ml
Butter	1/2 cup	125 ml
Milk	1 cup	250 ml
Rhubarb	2 cups	500 ml
Sugar	3/4 cup	175 ml
Flour	3 tbsp	45 ml
Brown sugar	1 1/2 cups	375 ml

Mix first 7 ingredients as for biscuits - roll out to a rectangle. Spread with a little extra butter. Combine rhubarb, sugar and flour and spread over dough; roll up dough like cinnamon rolls. Slice into 12 rolls and place in a 9 x 13 inch pan. Mix brown sugar with 2 cups boiling water.
Pour over rolls.
Bake at 350° for 40-45 minutes.

Strawberry Rhubarb Coffee Cake

Sugar	2/3 cup	150 ml
Cornstarch	1/3 cup	75 ml
Chopped rhubarb	2 cups	500 ml
Sliced strawberries	2 cups	500 ml
Lemon juice	2 tbsp	30 ml
CAKE:		
Flour	3 cups	750 ml
Sugar	1 cup	250 ml
Baking Powder	1 tsp	5 ml
Baking soda	1 tsp	5 ml
Cold butter	1 cup	250 ml
Eggs	2	2
Buttermilk	1 cup	250 ml
Vanilla extract	1 tsp	5 ml
TOPPING:		
Brown sugar	1/4 cup	60 ml
Flour	1/2 cup	125 ml
Cold butter	3 tbsp	45 ml
Cinnamon	1 1/2 tsp	7 ml

In a saucepan, combine sugar and cornstarch; stir in rhubarb and strawberries. Bring to a boil over medium heat; cook for 2 minutes or until thickened. Remove from the heat; stir in lemon juice. Cool.

For cake, combine flour, sugar, baking powder and baking soda in a large bowl. Cut in butter until mixture resembles coarse crumbs. Beat the eggs, buttermilk and vanilla; stir into crumb mixture just until moistened. Spoon two thirds of the batter into a greased 13 x 9 x 2 inch baking pan. Spoon cooled filling over batter. Top with remaining batter.

For topping, combine sugar, flour and cinnamon. Cut in butter until mixture resembles coarse crumbs; sprinkle over batter. Bake at 350° for 45-50 minutes or until golden brown. Cool on a wire rack.

Double Dipped Strawberries

Chocolate chips	1/2 cup	125 ml
White chocolate chips	1/2 cup	125 ml

Melt chips in microwave 'separately' for 1 1/2 - 2 minutes on medium power. Hold stems of berries and dip in dark chocolate 2/3rds of the way up the berry, lay on baking sheet. When dry, dip in melted white chocolate half way up the dark chocolate and lay on baking sheet.

See photo page 109.

Very Berry Chocolate Shortcake

Hulled and sliced strawberries	2 cups	500 ml
Sugar	1 cup	250 ml
Flour	2 cups	500 ml
Unsweetened cocoa powder	1/2 cup	125 ml
Baking Powder	1 tbsp	15 ml
Salt	1/2 tsp	2 ml
Butter	6 tbsp	90 ml
Milk	1/2 cup	125 ml
Vanilla	1 tsp	5 ml

Toss berries in a bowl with 1/4 cup of sugar, let stand for 20 minutes. Combine flour, cocoa, remaining sugar (3/4 cup), baking powder and salt. With pastry blender, cut in butter until mixture looks crumbly. Add milk and vanilla until mixture comes together.

Turn out on floured surface. Knead lightly 10 times. Pat to 3/4 inch thickness. Cut out shortcakes. Bake at 425° for 12 minutes.

To assemble, cool shortbread biscuits. Cut in half - put berries on bottom half, cover with whipped cream, add top half of biscuit. Add more berries and Rich Chocolate Sauce (page 152).

See photo page 109.

Strawberry Pie

Sugar	1/2 cup	125 ml
Flour	1/3 cup	75 ml
Sliced Strawberries	4 cups	1000 ml
Lemon juice	1 tbsp	15 ml
Butter	2 tbsp	30 ml
Pie crusts	2 - 9"	2 - 22 cm

Mix sugar and flour. Stir in hulled, sliced strawberries. Turn into unbaked pie shell which has been placed in pie plate. Sprinkle with lemon juice and dot with butter.

Cover with top crust, be sure to have slits in the top. Sprinkle top crust with sugar. Bake at 425° for 35-45 minutes. Cover edges of crust with foil - remove foil during the last 15 minutes of baking.

See photo page 109.

121

Strawberry Cream Cheese Pie

Dream Whip	1 pkg	1 pkg
Milk	1/2 cup	125 ml
Vanilla	1/2 tsp	2 ml
Cream cheese	8 oz	250 g
Sugar	1/2 cup	125 ml
Strawberry Jello	1 pkg	1 pkg
Boiling water	1 cup	250 ml
Sliced, sweetened strawberries	4 cups	1000 ml
Baked pie crust	1 - 9"	1 - 22 cm

　　Prepare whipped topping; in a separate bowl, whip cream cheese with sugar and mix these two together. Put into baked pie shell.
　　Dissolve jello in boiling water. Drain berries, reserving syrup and adding cold water, if necessary, to make 1/2 cup. Add berries and juice to jello, chill until partially thickened. Pour over cream cheese mixture. Chill at least 3 hours. Top with whipped cream when serving.

Easy Strawberry Pie

Baked pie crust	1 - 9"	1 - 22cm
Hulled, sliced strawberries	5 cups	1250 ml
Sugar	3/4 cup	175 ml
Cornstarch	2 tbsp	30 ml
Salt	pinch	pinch
Water	1/2 cup	125 ml
Cold water	2 tbsp	30 ml

　　Place 4 cups of the sliced strawberries in pie shell. Crush the remaining 1 cup of strawberries very fine. Heat sugar with water until sugar dissolves. Add to crushed berries, add salt, bring to a boil.
　　Mix cornstarch with cold water and add to hot mixture, stirring constantly. Cook slowly until thick and clear (about 10 minutes).
　　Cool slightly and pour over berries that are in the pie shell. Serve with whipped cream.

Strawberry Salmon Salad

Salmon steaks	4	4
Sour cream	1/2 cup	125 ml
Horseradish	1 tbsp	30 ml
Garlic salt	1/4 tsp	1 ml
Mixed salad greens	8 cups	2000 ml
Sliced strawberries	2 cups	500 ml
Balsamic vinegar	2 tbsp	30 ml

When preparing the salmon for this salad you may either season and barbeque the salmon steaks or, boil in 4 cups of water until they easily flake. Following either form of cooking, break salmon steaks into pieces.

In a bowl, stir sour cream, horseradish and garlic salt. Put greens and strawberries in salad bowl, drizzle with vinegar; add salmon pieces on top. Save sour cream mixture until serving time and use as dressing.

Cheesecake Dipped Strawberries

Cream cheese	4 oz	125 g
Sour cream	1/3 cup	75 ml
Icing sugar	3 tbsp	45 ml
Milk	1 tbsp	15 ml
Almond flavouring	1/4 tsp	1 ml
Graham wafer crumbs	1/4 cup	60 ml
Whole strawberries	2 cups	500 ml

Beat cream cheese till smooth; add sour cream, sugar, milk and almond flavouring. Mix well. Dip strawberries into cheesecake mixture then redip into wafer crumbs.

See photo page 109.

"Does anything taste as good as veggies picked in your own backyard? Summer Savoury features over 250 recipes and will inspire gardening chefs to create some mouthwatering dishes using homegrown vegetables and fruits."   *Gardenwise Magazine*

Summertime Veggie Pie

Ingredient	Imperial	Metric
All purpose flour	3/4 cup	175 ml
Whole wheat flour	3/4 cup	175 ml
Salt	1/2 tsp	2 ml
Ice water	1/4 cup	60 ml
Butter	1/2 cup	125 ml
Corn oil	2 tbsp	30 ml
Chopped onion	1 sm	1 sm
Minced garlic	2 cloves	2 cloves
Chopped celery	3 stalks	3 stalks
Sliced zucchini	2	2
Shredded carrots	1/2 cup	125 ml
Sliced mushrooms	1/2 cup	125 ml
Peas	1/2 cup	125 ml
Corn kernels	1/2 cup	125 ml
Honey	1 tbsp	15 ml
Dry mustard	1 tsp	5 ml
Salt	1/2 tsp	2 ml
Pepper	1/4 tsp	1 ml
Minced sage	1 tbsp	15 ml
Tomatoes	3	3
Shredded swiss cheese	1 cup	250 ml
Parsley	1 tbsp	15 ml

Make crust by sifting flours and 1/2 tsp salt together in a large bowl. Cut in butter until it resembles corn meal. Blend in water one tablespoon at a time until dough holds together. On a floured board, knead dough a few times and then pat it into a thick patty or disc. Place in baggie or wrap in plastic wrap and put in refrigerator for one hour or until ready to use.

Preheat oven to 375°. Place corn oil in a large skillet over medium low heat. Add garlic, onion and celery. Sauté for 5-10 minutes or until onion is tender. Stir in zucchini, carrots and mushrooms. Continue cooking for another 5-10 minutes or until vegetables are tender. Stir in peas and corn and cook for another 5 minutes. Stir in honey, mustard, salt, pepper and sage; remove from heat.

Press lightly against vegetable mixture to drain out any excess liquid and discard extra liquid. Roll out crust to fit a 9 inch pie plate or quiche dish. Place crust in dish and trim edges, then crimp. Prick bottom with fork and brush with milk or egg wash if desired.

Spoon vegetable mixture into prepared crust. Cover with tomatoes which have been seeded, stemmed, salted, strained and chopped. Add cheese and sprinkle with parsley. Brush crust edge with milk or egg wash. Bake for 45-50 minutes. Let stand 5-10 minutes before cutting.

Hint! Save cooking liquid from boiling vegetables; store in fridge. This makes a great stock for soups or stews.

Vegetable Quesadillas

Light cream cheese	4 oz	125 g
Chopped green onion	1/4 cup	125 ml
Seeded, diced tomato	1 lg	1 lg
Seeded, chopped sweet pepper	1	1
Grated cheddar cheese	1 1/2 cups	375 ml
Salsa	1/3 cup	75 ml
Tortillas	6 (8-10")	6 (20-25cm)

Combine green onion, tomato and sweet pepper. Spread cream cheese on half of each tortilla to 1/2 inch from edge. Sprinkle salsa on top of the cream cheese and then the combined vegetables. Top with grated cheese.

Fold uncovered half over filling. Press edges lightly with your hand to seal. Arrange on ungreased baking sheet (or electric grill). Bake at 425° for 10-15 minutes. Cut each into 4 wedges. Serve with Sour cream, Ranch dressing, Salsa or a dipping sauce of your choice.

ALTERNATE VEGGIE FILLING:

Corn	2 med ears	2 med ears
Yellow squash	2 med	2 med
Sliced sweet onion	1/2 sm	.5 sm
Fresh basil or	1 tbsp	15 ml
Dried basil	1/2 tsp	2 ml
Fresh oregano or	1 1/2 tsp	7 ml
Dried oregano	1/4 tsp	1 ml
Minced garlic	1 clove	1 clove
Salt/Pepper	to taste	to taste
Shredded Monterey Jack	1 cup	250 ml

Grill corn, covered, over medium heat for 10 minutes; turn. Place squash (halved lengthways) and onions on grill, cover and cook 10 minutes, turning once. When cool enough, remove kernels from cobs, chop squash and onions. Place in large bowl and stir in spices.

Follow instructions as above substituting this mixture for the combined vegetables shown above; using Monterey Jack instead of cheddar.

Hint! When you are preparing vegetable dishes, save the peelings, tips of beans, broccoli stems, etc. Put in a plastic bag in fridge. When bag is full, put contents of bag in water and boil for an hour or so. Strain the liquid and save as a wonderful stock.

Veggie Packed Pizza Pockets

Margarine	2 tbsp	30 ml
Diced onion	1 med	1 med
Diced green pepper	1 med	1 med
Sliced mushrooms	4	4
Diced zucchini	1/2 med	.5 med
Chopped broccoli florets	1/2 cup	125 ml
Spaghetti sauce	1/2 cup	125 ml
Shredded mozzarella	1 cup	250 ml
Pizza dough	1 pkg	1 pkg

Preheat oven to 400°. Grease two baking sheets. Melt margarine in skillet over medium heat. Add onion and pepper. Cook, stirring, for five minutes or until softened. Add mushrooms, zucchini and broccoli and continue to cook, stirring, for another 5 minutes. Stir in the spaghetti sauce and cook 1 - 2 minutes.

Lay pizza dough on a lightly floured surface and cut into 6 inch circles. In the center of each circle place 2 tbsp shredded cheese. Top cheese with about 1/4 cup of the veggie/sauce mixture. Brush edges of dough with a bit of water, fold in half, then roll and pinch edges together. Place pockets on baking sheet. Bake for 15-20 minutes or until lightly browned on top and bottom. Let cool slightly before serving. Makes 8 pockets.

On The Side

1. Brown Sugar Glazed Sprouts, page 26
2. Sweet Roasted Parsnips/Carrots, page 62
3. Three Pepper Veggie Toss, page 68
4. Sweet and Sour Potatoes, page 78

Presented in a variety of Paderno cookware, page 159.

Flower arrangement:

Celosia, Cosmos 'Cosmic Yellow, Gaillardia, Zinnia; using an acorn squash as a vase.

Toasted Veggie Sandwiches

Spicy brown mustard	4 tsp	20 ml
Split English muffins	4	4
Chopped broccoli	1/2 cup	125 ml
Chopped cauliflower	1/2 cup	125 ml
Chopped green pepper	1/2 cup	125 ml
Shredded cheddar cheese	1 cup	250 ml

Spread mustard on cut sides of English muffins. Top each with finely chopped vegetables and cheese. Broil 4 to 6 inches from heat for 3 minutes or until cheese is melted. Makes 4 servings.

Hint!   For a unique method of cooking corn, Place peeled corn in a pot of cold water with 1 tbsp sugar and 1 tbsp lemon juice. Bring to a full boil and boil for 2 minutes uncovered. Remove from heat, cover and let stand for 10 minutes.

Church Pot Luck

1. Egg Plant Bake, page 48
2. Mustard Pickles, page 47
3. Beet Relish, page 16
4. Meatless Meatloaf, page 65
5. Broccoli and Corn Bake, page 22

Flower arrangement:

Feathertop Grass, Maiden Grass 'Morning Light', Alternanthera 'Purple Knight'.

Cheesy Vegetable Moussaka

Eggplant	1 lg	500 g
Coarse cooking salt	dash	dash
Olive oil	6 tbsp	90 ml
Butter	4 tbsp	90 ml
Peeled, sliced potatoes	2 lg	600 g
Crushed garlic	4 cloves	4 cloves
Chopped onions	2 med	300 g
Grated zucchini	2 med	240 g
Grated carrots	2 med	240 g
Chopped, crushed tomatoes	2 1/2 cups	625 ml
Sliced mushrooms	1 cup	250 ml
Tomato paste	1 tbsp	15 ml
Dry red wine	1/4 cup	60 ml
Sugar	1 tsp	5 ml
Grated old cheddar	1/3 cup	75 ml

CHEESE SAUCE:

Butter	1 1/2 oz	40 g
Flour	1/4 cup	60 ml
Milk	1 3/4 cups	425 ml
Grated parmesan	1 cup	250 ml
Lightly beaten egg	1	1

Grease shallow ovenproof dish (10 cup capacity). Cut eggplant into slices, place slices on wire rack or in colander, sprinkle with salt; let stand 30 minutes. Rinse eggplant under water; drain on paper towel. Place slices in single layer on oven trays, grill on both sides until lightly browned; drain on paper towel.

Heat 4 tbsp oil and butter in pan, add potatoes in batches, cook until well browned on both sides; drain on absorbent paper. Heat remaining 2 tbsp oil in pan, add garlic and onions, stirring, until onions are soft. Add zucchini and carrots, cook, stirring, 5 minutes. Stir in crushed tomatoes, mushrooms, paste, wine and sugar; simmer, uncovered about 20 minutes or until thickened. Place half the eggplant over base of prepared dish, top with half the potatoes and half the tomato mixture. Repeat with remaining eggplant, potatoes and tomato mixtures. Top with cheese sauce, sprinkle with cheddar cheese. Bake in moderately hot oven about 25 minutes or until browned and heated through.

Cheese Sauce: Heat butter in pan, add flour, stir until bubbling. Remove from heat, gradually stir in milk, stir over heat until mixture boils and thickens. Remove from heat, stir in cheese, cool 5 minutes. Stir in egg; stir until smooth.

Rainbow Veggie Casserole

Potatoes	8 med	8 med
Butter	4 tbsp	60 ml
Sour cream	1 cup	250 ml
Salt	1 tsp	5 ml
Torn, fresh spinach	1 1/2 cups	375 ml
Sliced green onions	2	2
Crushed, minced garlic	2 cloves	2 cloves
Lightly beaten egg	1	1
Cooked squash	1 1/2 cups	375 ml
Dried ginger	1/4 tsp	1 ml
Grated cheddar cheese	1 cup	250 ml

Peel potatoes, cut in half and cook in boiling water until tender. Drain and mash. Stir in 2 tbsp of butter, sour cream and 1/2 tsp salt. Put spinach in a medium bowl. Stir in garlic, green onions, egg, 1 tbsp butter and 1/4 tsp salt. Drain any liquid off the cooked squash. Stir in the final 1 tbsp of butter, ginger and the remaining 1/4 tsp of salt. Grease an 8 cup casserole. Spoon 1/3 of the potato mixture into the casserole. Smooth flat. Spread all of the squash mixture over the potatoes in the casserole. Spread half of the remaining potato mixture on top of the squash. Smooth flat. Spread all of the spinach mixture, and finally, spread the last of the potaato mixture on top. Sprinkle with cheese. Bake, uncovered at 350° for 55-65 minutes.

Veggies with Maple Ginger Glaze

Peeled and cut parsnips	1/2 lb	500 g
Peeled and cut carrots	1/2 lb	500 g
Peeled and cut turnip	1/2 lb	500 g
Brussel sprouts	1/2 lb	500 g
Fresh ginger	1/3 cup	75 ml
Unsalted butter	3 tbsp	45 ml
Salt	to taste	to taste
Black pepper	to taste	to taste
Grated fresh ginger	1 tsp	5 ml
Maple syrup	1 1/2 tbsp	22 ml

Cut parsnips, carrots into 2" by 1/2 " sticks; cut turnip into thin wedges; trim and halve sprouts; peel and thinly slice a 2" piece of ginger into matchstick sized pieces. Heat oven to 425°. Spread the vegetables and the ginger matchsticks in a large, low-sided pan. Drizzle with the butter and season with salt and pepper. Toss to evenly coat the veggies and spread them so they are just one layer deep. Roast the vegetables, tossing a couple of times, until tender and golden brown in spots, about 30 minutes. Combine the grated ginger and maple syrup; drizzle the vegetables with mixture, toss and roast an additional 5 minutes.

Four Layer Veggie Loaf

Grated carrot	1 1/2 cups	375 ml
Orange juice	2 tbsp	30 ml
Beaten eggs	4	4
Bread crumbs	8 tbsp	120 ml
Chopped cauliflower	1 sm head	1 sm head
Mustard	1 tsp	5 ml
Grated cheese	1/4 cup	60 ml
Mashed peas (cooled)	1 cup	250 ml
Mashed potatoes (cooled)	2 cups	500 ml
Butter	1 tbsp	15 ml
Milk	2 tbsp	30 ml

Mix carrot and orange juice, place in bottom of greased loaf pan; cover with 1 beaten egg and 2 tbsp of bread crumbs along with dash of salt and pepper.

Mix cauliflower, mustard and cheese. Place over carrot layer and cover with another layer of the egg/crumb/seasoning mixture. Place peas over cauliflower, cover again with egg mixture.

Finally cover peas with mashed potatoes that have been creamed with butter and milk. Top with remaining portion of egg, crumb and seasonings. Sprinkle with paprika. Bake at 350° for one hour. Let set a few minutes, turn out on platter.

Barbequed Veggie Packets

Onions, sliced or wedges	2 med	2 med
Carrots, peeled, cut in sticks	4 med	4 med
New potatoes, scrubbed	4 sm	4 sm
Seeded, sliced peppers	2	2
Lemon juice	1-2 tsp	5-10 ml

Spray two sheets of heavy duty aluminum foil with vegetable spray. On each sheet, lay half the carrots, onions, peppers and potatoes. Sprinkle each with 1 tbsp of water and 1-2 tsp lemon juice.

Wrap up making sure packet is sealed well. Place on low/medium heat grill; veggie packets will be done in approximately 20 minutes.

Delicious and no pots to clean! Be creative with your choice of veggies.

Hint!   When needing to chop green onions, it's much easier to use a pair of clean scissors instead of a knife.

Barbeque Salad Dressing

Mayonnaise	1/2 cup	125 ml
Barbeque sauce	1/4 cup	60 ml
Onion flakes	1 tbsp	15 ml
Lemon juice	1 tbsp	15 ml
Salt	dash	dash
Pepper	dash	dash

Mix all ingredients and refrigerate. Stir or shake before serving.

Versatile Salad Dressing

Soft tofu	1/2 cup	125 ml
Balsamic vinegar	3 tbsp	45 ml
Olive oil	1/4 cup	60 ml
Garlic	1-2	1-2
Fresh parsley	1 tbsp	15 ml
Salt	to taste	to taste

In a food processor, blend the tofu, oil and vinegar. Fold in other ingredients; cover and refrigerate for 2 days. If oil separates, whisk before serving. You may also add honey, feta cheese and tarragon if so desired.

Flax Oil Salad Dressing

Lemon (juice only)	1	1
Flax oil	4 tbsp	60 ml
Soy sauce	1 tsp	5 ml
Minced onion	2 tbsp	30 ml
Finely grated carrots	2 tbsp	30 ml
Salad herbs	to taste	to taste

Mix all ingredients and refrigerate. Stir or shake before serving.

Hint!   Add firm (grated) tofu to any salad dressing mixture for extra protein.

Spicy Citrus Dressing

Lemon juice	1/4 cup	125 ml
Honey	2 tbsp	30 ml
Oil	1 tbsp	15 ml
Cinnamon	1/4 tsp	1 ml
Allspice	1/4 tsp	1 ml
Paprika	1/8 tsp	.5 ml

Mix all ingredients and refrigerate. Stir or shake before serving.

Italian Salad Dressing

Soft tofu	4 oz	125 g
Buttermilk	1/3 cup	75 ml
Vinegar	2 tbsp	30 ml
Dry mustard	1/4 tsp	1 ml
Garlic	to taste	to taste
Italian seasoning	to taste	to taste

Blend in food processor. Refrigerate for at least 2 hours or up to 48 hours.

Maple Salad Dressing

Maple Syrup	1 cup	250 ml
Oil	2 tbsp	30 ml
Lemon juice	1 tbsp	15 ml
Paprika	1/2 tsp	2 ml
Salt	1/4 tsp	1 ml
Dry mustard	1/4 tsp	1 ml
Onion powder	1/4 tsp	1 ml

Mix all ingredients and refrigerate. Stir or shake before serving.

Green Salad Dressing

Olive oil	2/3 cup	150 ml
Cider vinegar	1/3-1/2 cup	75-125 ml
Parmesan	2 tbsp	30 ml
Sugar	1 tsp	5 ml
Garlic	1 clove	1 clove
Basil	1/4 tsp	1 ml
Oregano	1/4 tsp	1 ml
Parsley	1/2 tsp	2 ml
Salt	to taste	to taste
Pepper	to taste	to taste

Mix all ingredients and refrigerate. Stir or shake before serving. Goes perfectly with the Three Green Salad found on page 54.

Golden Green Bean Salad Dressing

Chopped, hard cooked egg	1	1
Minced onion	1 tbsp	15 ml
Cider vinegar	1/4 cup	60 ml
Oil	1/2 cup	125 ml
Salt	1/2 tsp	2 ml
Curry powder	1/8 tsp	.5 ml

Mix all ingredients and refrigerate. Stir or shake before serving. Goes particularly well with the Summer Green Bean Salad found on page 15.

Spinach Salad Soybean Oil Dressing

Soybean oil	2/3 cup	150 ml
Cider vinegar	1/4 cup	60 ml
Orange juice	2 tbsp	30 ml
Finely chopped shallots	1 tbsp	15 ml
Grated gingeroot	3/4 tsp	3 ml
Thyme	3/4 tsp	3 ml
Pepper	to taste	to taste
Salt	to taste	to taste

Mix all ingredients and refrigerate. Stir or shake before serving.

Vinaigrette

Olive oil	1/2 cup	125 ml
Red wine vinegar	1/4 cup	60 ml
Sugar	2 tbsp	30 ml
Minced garlic	1 clove	1 clove
Tabasco	dash	dash
Salt	to taste	to taste
Pepper	to taste	to taste

Mix well and refrigerate in a mason jar. Shake before using.

Simple, Simple Salad Dressing

Granulated sugar	1/4 cup	60 ml
Vegetable oil	1/4 cup	60 ml
White vinegar	1/4 cup	60 ml

Mix well and refrigerate.

Delicious Poppy Seed Dressing

Maple syrup	1 cup	250 ml
Mayonnaise	1 cup	250 ml
Finely chopped garlic	2 tbsp	30 ml
Dijon mustard	1/4 cup	60 ml
Poppy seeds	3 tbsp	45 ml

Mix well and refrigerate.

See photo front cover.

Caesar Salad Dressing

Chopped garlic	2 cloves	2 cloves
Mazola oil	1/2 cup	125 ml
Worcestershire sauce	1 tsp	5 ml
Salt	3/4 tsp	3 ml
Ground black pepper	1/8 tsp	.5 ml
Dry mustard	1/4 tsp	1 ml
Egg yolk	1	1
Lemon juice	2 tsp	10 ml
White vinegar	2 tsp	10 ml
Parmesan cheese	1/3 cup	75 ml

Mix all ingredients well and refrigerate until needed.

Salad Greens Dressing

White wine vinegar	1/4 cup	60 ml
Orange juice	1/4 cup	60 ml
Granulated sugar	1 tbsp	15 ml
Dijon mustard	1 tsp	5 ml
Salt	1/2 tsp	2 ml
Pepper	1/2 tsp	2 ml
Extra virgin olive oil	1/2 cup	125 ml

Makes 1 cup of dressing. Make ahead and refrigerate in an airtight jar for up to 5 days. Shake well before using.

Asparagus Orange Mayonnaise

Yogurt	2 tbsp	30 ml
Mayonnaise	2 tbsp	30 ml
Grated orange peel	1 orange	1 orange

Mix all ingredients together. Perfect for serving on cooked asparagus.

Parma Dip

Miracle whip	1 cup	250 ml
Parmesan cheese	1/4 cup	60 ml
Milk	1/4 cup	60 ml
Chives	1 tbsp	15 ml

Combine and mix well. Chill.

Deluxe Lobster Dip

Lobster paste	3 oz can	
Cream cheese	8 oz	85g can
Mayonnaise	1/2 cup	250 g
French dressing	3 tbsp	125 ml
Chopped onion	1 tbsp	45 ml
Seasonings	to taste	15 ml
		to taste

Beat cheese, then add and beat mayonnaise, French dressing, onion and seasonings. Lastly, add lobster paste. Chill.

Curry Dip

Mayonnaise	1 cup	250 ml
Sour cream	1/2 cup	125 ml
Lemon juice	1 tbsp	15 ml
Chives	1 tbsp	15 ml
Minced onion	1 tbsp	15 ml
Paprika	1/4 tsp	1 ml
Curry powder	1/8 tsp	.5 ml
Salt	1/4 tsp	1 ml
Garlic salt	1 tsp	5 ml
Worcestershire sauce	1/2 tsp	2 ml

Blend all ingredients until smooth. Refrigerate until serving.

See photo page 38.

Citrus Fruit Dip

Eggs	2	2
Sugar	1/2 cup	125 ml
Lemon juice	1/4 cup	60 ml
Orange juice	1/4 cup	60 ml
Plain yogurt	6 oz	170 g
Vanilla	1 tsp	5 ml

Beat eggs slightly; beat in sugar, lemon juice and orange juice and vanilla. Microwave on high for 2 1/2 minutes or until it boils and thickens. Stir every 30 seconds. Cover surface with Saran wrap. Cool. Fold in yogurt and vanilla. Spoon over a fruit cup.

Faye's Vegetable Dip

Mayonnaise	1 cup	250 ml
Chili sauce	2 tsp	10 ml
Grated onion	2 tsp	10 ml
Vinegar	2 tsp	10 ml
Salt	1/2 tsp	2 ml
Curry	1/2 tsp	2 ml

Combine all ingredients; refrigerate.

Eleanor's Vegetable Dip

Miracle Whip	1 cup	250 ml
Ketchup	4 tbsp	60 ml
Garlic	to taste	to taste
Curry	1/2 tsp	2 ml
Worcestershire sauce	2 tsp	10 ml
Lemon juice	2 tsp	10 ml
Onion salt	1 tsp	5 ml

Combine all ingredients; refrigerate.

Cottage Cheese Dill Dip

Cottage Cheese	1 cup	250 ml
Green onion	1	1
Parsley	2 tsbp	30 ml
Fresh dill	1 tbsp	15 ml
Worcestershire sauce	1/2 tsp	2 ml
Salt	to taste	to taste
Pepper	to taste	to taste
Garlic	to taste	to taste

In blender, blend cottage cheese and other ingredients. Refrigerate at least one hour.

Carrot Dip

Sliced, peeled carrots	3	3
Brown sugar	1 tbsp	15 ml
Chopped chives	1 stalk	1 stalk
Mashed garlic	1 clove	1 clove
Olive oil	1 tbsp	15 ml

Cook carrots in water with garlic until tender. Remove from heat and cool. Blend in food processor; adding chives, brown sugar and oil. Add extra water if too thick. Place in bowl; refrigerate.

Great with nacho chips or crackers.

See photo page 38.

Baked Asparagus Dip

Finely chopped cooked asparagus	1 lb	500 g
Grated parmesan	1 cup	250 ml
Mayonnaise	1 cup	250 ml

Blend asparagus with cheese and mayonnaise. Place in casserole and bake at 375° for 20 minutes. Serve hot with crackers.

Greek Dip

2% milk	1/2 cup	125 ml
1% cottage cheese	1/2 cup	125 ml
Crumbled feta cheese	1/2 cup	125 ml
Dried oregano	1 tsp	5 ml
Grated lemon peel	1/4 tsp	1 ml
Pepper	to taste	to taste

Blend until smooth. Refrigerate.

Easy Fruit Dip

Vanilla yogurt	1 1/2 cups	375 ml
Flaked coconut	4 1/2 tsp	22 ml
Orange marmalade	4 1/2 tsp	22 ml

Mix all ingredients, refrigerate.

Creamy Vegetable Dip

Hellman's mayonnaise	1 cup	250 ml
Sour cream	1 cup	250 ml
Parsley	1 tsp	5 ml
Dill seed	1 tsp	5 ml
Celery seed	1 tsp	5 ml
Chopped green peppers	1 tbsp	15 ml
Garlic salt	1/2 tsp	2 ml
Tabasco	2 drops	2 drops
Accent	1 tsp	5 ml

Mix all ingredients together, cover and refrigerate before serving. This dip will keep well for a few days.

See photo page 38.

Parmesan Cheese Veggie Dip

Miracle Whip	1/3 cup	75 ml
Hellman's mayonnaise	2/3 cup	150 ml
Milk	1 tbsp	15 ml
Dry mustard	1/4-1/2 tsp	1-2 ml
Garlic salt	dash	dash
Lemon juice	1 tsp	5 ml
Parmesan cheese	3 tbsp	45 ml

Mix together and chill well before using.

Baked Potato Stuffing

Butter	1/4 cup	60 ml
Chopped onion	1 med	1 med
Plain yogurt	12 oz	375 g
Dill weed	to taste	to taste
Baked potatoes	4	4

   Bake 4 potatoes; cut top 1/3 off baked potato and remove the inside. Lightly mash the contents you have removed and combine with other ingredients. Before stuffing the empty potato skin, season the inside of the shell with salt and pepper. Place in 350° oven for 15 minutes.

Beef Stuffing

Lean ground beef	1 lb	500 g
Chopped onion	1 med	1 med
Cooked, crumbled bacon	6 strips	6 strips
Sour cream	1/2 cup	125 ml
Shredded cheddar	1/4 cup	60 ml
Milk	1/4 cup	60 ml
Baking potatoes	4	4
Butter	2 tbsp	30 ml
Salt	to taste	to taste

   Bake potatoes. Cut top 1/3 off and scoop out pulp. Cook beef and onion; let cool about 10 minutes. Mix potato pulp with butter, salt and milk. Blend with cooked beef and onion mixture then add crumbled bacon, sour cream and additional salt. Spoon into empty potato shells and sprinkle with cheese. Bake at 400° for approximately 20 minutes.

Broccoli Stuffing

Cottage cheese	8 tbsp	120 ml
Chopped, cooked broccoli	1 cup	250 ml
Parmesan cheese	2 tbsp	30 ml
Pasta sauce	1 cup	250 ml
Baking potatoes	4	4

   Bake potatoes and remove inside pulp. Mix scooped out potato with cottage cheese. Stir in chopped broccoli and parmesan cheese. Place in potato shell. Top with heated pasta sauce and additional parmesan. Broil for 5 minutes.

Tasty Stuffing

Cream of chicken soup	1 can	1 can
Thyme	dash	dash
Dill	dash	dash
Parmesan cheese	1/2 cup	125 ml
Paprika	dash	dash
Baked potatoes	4	4

Cut top off baked potato and scoop out pulp, reserving the skins. Mash scooped out potato with cream of chicken soup, some thyme and dill. Fill potato skins and top with parmesan and paprika. Broil about 5 minutes.

Hot Milk Baked Potato Stuffing

Butter	1/4 cup	125 ml
Hot milk	1 cup	250 ml
Salt	1 tsp	5 ml
Black pepper	1/8 tsp	.5 ml
Grated cheddar cheese	1 cup	250 ml
Baked potatoes	4	4

Cut baked potatoes in half. Remove pulp. Put in large bowl. Add butter, hot milk, salt, pepper and cheese. Mash or beat well with an electric mixer. Fill potato skins. Bake at 350° until hot.

See photo page 73.

Summertime Brunch

1. Fruit Smoothie, page 150
2. Cheesy Broccoli Pie, page 24
3. Onion and Cheese Tarts, page 60
4. French Toast Bake, page 113

Flower arrangement:

Gerbera Living Colours, Zinnia 'Zig Zag', Geranium 'Ringo White'.

Basic Potato Stuffing

Butter	1/2 cup	125 ml
Sour cream	1 cup	250 ml
Bacon bits	4 tsp	20 ml
Chives	4 tsp	20 ml
Grated cheddar	1 cup	250 ml
Baked potatoes	4	4

Cut baked potatoes in half. Remove pulp. Mix first four ingredients with potato pulp. Fill skins. Sprinkle with cheese. Place in 350° oven until hot and cheese melts.

Soufflé Baked Potato Stuffing

Butter	3-4 tbsp	45-60 ml
Hot milk or cream	3 tbsp	45 ml
Salt	1 tsp	5 ml
Sautéed grated onion	2 tbsp	30 ml
Egg whites (whipped)	2	2
Grated hard cheese	1/2 cup	125 ml
Paprika	dash	dash
Baked potatoes	4	4

Cut baked potatoes in half. Remove pulp. Add first 5 ingredients to pulp; beat well. Stuff potatoes, sprinkle with paprika. Bake at 350° until hot.

Paderno Kitchen

1. Dutch Oven with Lid
2. Fry Pan
3. Saucepan
4. Double Boiler

For full selection, sizes and prices for Paderno Cookware, please see page 159.

Marmalade Glazed Carrots

Toss hot cooked carrot slices with butter and 1-2 tablespoons of marmalade until marmalade melts... simple yet very tasty!

Apple Glazed Carrots

Apple sauce	1/4 cup	60 ml
Brown sugar	3 tbsp	45 ml
Butter	1 1/2 tbsp	22 ml

Cook until brown sugar melts. Pour over carrots. Bake at 350° for 15 minutes.

See photo page 37.

Lemon Glazed Carrots

Lemon juice	1 tbsp	15 ml
Sugar	1/3 cup	75 ml
Water	1/2 cup	125 ml
Salt	1 tsp	5 ml
Butter	2 tbsp	30 ml

Cook in all ingredients in skillet; add cooked carrots sliced lengthwise and toss.

Orange Cranberry Glaze

Butter	1/4 cup	60 ml
Cranberry sauce	1/4 cup	60 ml
Grated orange rind	2 tsp	10 ml
Honey	2 tbsp	30 ml
Salt	to taste	to taste

Combine all ingredients in blender. Pour over cooked carrots and toss until covered.

Honeydew Lemonade

Peeled, seeded and cubed honeydew melon	1 med	1 med
Fresh lemon juice	1 cup	250 ml
Sugar	3/4 cup	175 ml
Water	2 cups	500 ml
Lemon zest	2 lemons	2 lemons

Combine lemon juice, zest and sugar in a small saucepan. Bring to a boil. Simmer until the sugar dissolves. Strain and cool.

Purée melon in a blender. Add the cooled lemon mixture to the melon purée in the blender. Refrigerate, when ready to serve, add the water. Blend well; pour over crushed ice. Garnish with lemon slices.

See photo page 91.

Raspberry Lemon Smoothie

Boiling water	2 cups	500 ml
Lemon herbal tea	7 bags	7 bags
Pineapple juice	1 3/4 cups	425 ml
Raspberry sherbet	1 pint	450 ml
Lemon juice	1/4 cup	60 ml

In a teapot, pour boiling water over tea bags; cover and leave for 5 minutes. Remove bags. Chill tea. In blender, process tea, pineapple juice, lemon juice and sherbet until smooth. Pour into 4 glasses and garnish with lemon slices if desired.

Fruit Smoothie

Strawberries	1 1/2 cups	375 ml
Banana	1 lg	1 lg
Yogurt	1 sm tub	1 sm tub
Blueberries	1/2 cup	125 ml
Orange juice	1 cup	250 ml

Mix in blender until smooth. Serve immediately. Leftovers will keep until later in the day, but must be blended again.

See photo page 145.

Refreshing Raspberry Cooler

Raspberries (thawed if frozen)	8 cups	2 lit
Sugar	1 1/2 cups	375 ml
Cider vinegar	2/3 cup	150 ml
Water	1/2 cup	125 ml
Chilled ginger ale	8 cups	2 lit
Cold water	2 cups	500 ml

In a large saucepan, crush the berries. Stir in sugar, vinegar and water. Bring to a boil; reduce heat. Simmer, uncovered, for 20 minutes. Strain to remove seeds; refrigerate. Just before serving, stir in ginger ale and cold water. Serve over ice. Makes about 3 1/2 quarts.

Blackberry Banana Smoothie

Orange juice	2 cups	500 ml
Vanilla yogurt	1/3 cup	75 ml
Bananas	2 med	2 med
Blackberries	1/2 cup	125 ml

In preparation for this smoothie, cut ripe bananas in thirds and freeze. Once frozen, mix all ingredients together in blender. Process until smooth. Serve immediately.

Tangy Fruit Punch

Pineapple juice	46 oz	1400 ml
Orange juice concentrate	12 oz	375 ml
Lemonade concentrate	3/4 cup	175 ml
Water	1 cup	250 ml
Sugar	1/2 cup	125 ml
Ripe bananas	2	2
Thawed frozen strawberries	20 oz	625 ml
Chilled ginger ale	8 cups	2000 ml

In a punch bowl or large container, combine pineapple juice, orange juice concentrate, lemonade concentrate, 1/2 cup water and sugar. Place bananas, strawberries and remaining water in blender; cover and process until smooth. Stir into juice mixture. Cover and refrigerate. Just before serving, stir in ginger ale. Makes 25-30 servings (about 5 quarts)

"Summer Savoury has a unique flair for all things retro - fun, old fashioned recipe ideas that harken back to family suppers and bake sales... it's full of favourites that inspire everyone to bring back the kitchen garden and turn the fruits (and vegetables) of your labour into classic home-style meals."
Catherine Therrien, Assistant Editor Gardening Life

151

Strawberry Lemonade

Cold water	3 cups	750 ml
Fresh Strawberries	5 cups	1250 ml
Sugar	3/4 cup	175 ml
Lemon juice	3/4 cup	175 ml
Cold club soda	2 cups	500 ml

Place water, strawberries and sugar in a blender; cover and process until smooth. Stir in lemon juice. Blend in soda; serve immediately. Garnish glasses with lemon slices if so desired. Makes 8 servings (10 cups).

See photo page 91.

Rich Chocolate Sauce

Butter	1 cup	250 ml
Unsweetened Chocolate	4 squares	4 squares
Sugar	3 cups	750 ml
Baking cocoa	1 cup	250 ml
Whipping cream	2 cups	500 ml
Vanilla extract	2 tsp	10 ml

In a heavy saucepan over low heat, melt butter and chocolate. Stir in sugar and cocoa until smooth. Gradually add cream; mix well. Cook for 10 minutes or until sugar is dissolved, stirring frequently. Remove from the heat; stir in vanilla. Serve over ice cream or any fruit dish you can imagine. Store leftover sauce in the refrigerator.

Watermelon Slice Cookies

Sugar	1 cup	250 ml
Butter (softened)	1 cup	250 ml
Cream cheese (softened)	3 oz pkg	85 g pkg
Salt	1/2 tsp	2 ml
Almond	1/2 tsp	2 ml
Vanilla	1/2 tsp	2 ml
Egg yolk	1	1
Flour	2 cups	500 ml

In a bowl, combine sugar, butter, cream cheese, salt, almond, vanilla and egg yolk; blend well. Stir in flour. Refrigerate dough for 2 hours.

Roll out dough, 1/3rd at a time on lightly floured board to 1/4 inch thickness. Cut into circles 2-3 inches in diameter. Cut circles in half to make watermelon wedges.

Bake at 375° for 7-10 minutes.

Make favourite white icing tinting some pink and some green. Ice cookies pink then edge with green. Use chocolate chips for watermelon seeds.

See photo page 110.

INDEX

Appetizers
Asparagus Rolls 9
Crunchy Cuke Rounds 46
Cucumber Canapes...............47
Onion and Cheese Tarts.........60
Show-off Melon Treat 32
Sweet Warm Onion Spread 58
Tomato Basil Squares 96
Tomato Salad Cups 99
Zucchini Dipsticks 106

Asparagus
Almond Orange Asparagus.........8
Asparagus Berry Salad 10
Asparagus Tart 8
Asparagus Rolls 9
Layered Asparagus.................9

Baking Beans
Maple Baked Beans 10
Rush Hour Beans...................11
Saturday Night Baked Beans 11

Beans
Beans and Veggie Primavera 14
Dill Beans 13
Green Beans with Onions 14
Herb, Pine Nut Green Beans 15
Simple Summer Beans............13
Summer Green Bean Salad.......15
Three Colour Bean Salad 12

Beets
Beet and Potato Mash 18
Beet Relish........................16
Beets Russian 16
Better Pickled Beets..............17
Harvard Beets 21
Orange Marinade for Beets.......21
Tasty Baked Beets 17

Blackberries
Black and Blue Cobbler 108
Cinnamon Choc. Fruit Cup......111
Dressed Up Blackberries 107

Blueberries
Blueberry Bundt Cake........114
Blueberry Oat Treats.........112
French Toast Bake............113
Lemon Blueberry Scones.....113
Peach Blueberry Crisp 112

Bonus Recipes
Rich Chocolate Sauce 152
Watermelon Slice Cookies...153

Breads and Muffins
Carrot Chocolate Chip Loaf...34
Carrot Pineapple Muffins 36
Cranberry S. Potato Muffins ..81
Island Potato Bannock.........79
Lemon Blueberry Scones.....113
Pumpkin Bread 85
Rhubarb Muffins..............119
S. Potato Banana Muffins 81
S. Potato Quick Bread 82
Sweet Potato Scones 83
Zucchini Carrot Muffins 102
Zucchini Choc. Chip Muffins 106

Broccoli
Broccoli and Cauliflower Bake ...23
Broccoli and Corn Bake 22
Broccoli Slaw Salad 24
Broccoli Vegetable Pie 22
Cheesy Broccoli Pie 24
Scrumptious Broccoli Salad...23

Brussels Sprouts
Brown Sugar Glazed Sprouts..26
Brussells Sprouts Casserole ..26
Delicious Brussels Sprouts 25
Lemon Glazed Sprouts........25

Cabbage
Cabbage and Apple Treat.....29
Cabbage Tomato Stir Fry 30
Cheddar Cabbage Casserole ..28
Honey Mustard Slaw 28
Red Cabbage with Apples.....29
Stuffed Cabbage Rolls 27
Surprise Coleslaw 30

Cantaloupe
Cantaloupe Fruit Cup..........32
Cantaloupe Fruit Toss 31
Cantaloupe Special 31
Show-off Melon Treat 32

Carrot Glazes
Apple Glazed Carrots 148
Lemon Glazed Carrots 148
Marmalaade Glazed Carrots 148
Orange Cranberry Glaze 148

Carrots
Carrot Pineapple Muffins 36
Carrot Burgers 39
Carrot Chocolate Chip Loaf...34
Carrot Country Pie.............33
Cream of Carrot Soup 33

Carrots
Hidden Surprise Carrot Cake 35
Sweet and Sour Carrots 34

Cauliflower
Faye's Mom's Cauliflower 40
Missouri Soup 40
Cauliflower Pie 41
Turk's dish 41

Celery
Cream of Celery Soup 42
Waldorf Salad..................... 42

Corn
Corn Chowder 43
Corn with Savoury Lime Butter .. 43
Roasted Corn and Garlic Rice 45
Salmon Corn Chowder............ 44
Spicy Corn Spread 44
Succotash 45
Sweet Corn Toss 44

Cucumber
Alice's Lime Cucumber Salad 46
Cruncy Cuke Rounds 46
Cucumber Canapes................ 47
Cucumber Veggie Salad 48
Mustard Pickles 47

Desserts
Black and Blue Cobbler 108
Blueberry Bundt Cake........... 114
Blueberry Oat Treats............ 112
Butternut Apple Crisp 94
Cantaloupe Fruit Cup 32
Cheesecake Dipped S.berries ... 123
Chocolate Topped Fruit Cups ... 114
Cinnamon Chocolate Fruit Tart . 111
Double Dipped Strawberries 120
Dressed Up Blackberries 107
Easy Strawberry pie 122
Hidden Surprise Carrot Cake 35
Honey Pumpkin Pie............... 87
Kiwi Strawberry Dessert 115
Lorraine's Pumpkin Cake........ 84
Melon Blueberry Treat 102
Peach Blueberry Crisp 112
Pumpkin Cake Roll 86
Pumpkin Pie for Dr. Jim......... 85
Raspberry Cheesecake.......... 117
Raspberry Orange Swirls 116
Rhubarb Cereal Crisp 118
Rhubarb Peach Pie 118

Desserts
Rhubarb Pinwheels 119
S.berry Cream Cheese Pie... 122
Strawberry Pie 121
S.berry Rhubarb Coffee Cake 120
Sweet Potato Layer Cake 80
Upside Down S. Potato Cake . 84
Very Berry Choc. Shortcake . 121
White Chocolate Fruit Tart . 115
Zucchini Carrot Cake......... 105
Zucchini Chocolate Cake 104

Dips
Baked Asparagus Dip 141
Carrot Dip..................... 140
Cirus Fruit Dip................. 139
Cottage Cheese Dill Dip...... 140
Creamy Vegetable Dip 142
Curry Dip...................... 138
Deluxe Lobster Dip 138
Easy Fruit Dip 141
Eleanor's Vegetable Dip 139
Faye's Vegetable Dip......... 139
Greek Dip 141
Parma Dip..................... 138
Parmesan Cheese Veg Dip ... 142

Drinks
Bkberry/Banana Smoothie .. 151
Fruit Smoothie 150
Honeydew Lemonade 149
Raspberry/Lemon Smoothie 149
Raspberry Cooler 150
Strawberry lemonade 152
Tangy Fruit Punch 151

Eggplant
Eggplant Bake 48
Eggplant French Fries 50
Eggplant Parmesan............. 50
Eggplant Pockets 49
Stuffed Eggplant 49

Kale
Kale and Squash Pie 51

Kiwi
Choc. Topped Fruit Cups 114
Kiwi Strawberry Dessert 115
White Choc. Fruit Tart....... 115

Leek
Leek and Potato Soup 53
Leek/Egg/Cheese Strata 53
Pork Chops and Leeks 52

INDEX

Leek
Scottish Leek Broth...............52
Lettuce
Three Green Salad 54
Lima Beans
Barbequed Lima Beans...........12
Mixed Vegetables
Barbequed Veggie Packets 132
Cheesy Vegetable Moussaka 130
Four Layer Veggie Loaf 132
Rainbow Veggie Casserole 131
Summertime Veggie Pie 124
Toasted Veggie Sandwiches 129
Vegetable Quesadillas 125
Veggie Packed Pizza Pockets ...126
Veggies/Maple Ginger Glaze....131
Okra
Okra, Wax Bean Salad 57
Onion
Caramelized Onions 60
Chop Suey 61
Creamed Onions 59
Onion and Apple Casserole.......59
Onion and Cheese Tarts 60
Onion Chicken Fried Rice 58
Onion Spread 58
Oriental Vegetable Delight.......61
Parsnip
French Parsnips...................63
Parsnip Patties...................64
Parsnip Turnip Casserole 62
Parsnip Veggie Roast 63
Sweet Roasted Parsnips/Carrots.62
Peas
Bubble and Squeak 65
Creamed Peas on Toast 64
Meatless Meat Loaf 65
Snow Peas and Peppers 66
Snow Pea Blend 66
Peppers
Pepperonata 68
Red Pepper Barley Casserole 69
Stuffed Green Peppers 67
Three Pepper Veggie Toss 68
Pies
Carrot Country Pie 33
Cheesy Broccoli Pie..............24
Easy Strawberry Pie 122
Honey Pumpkin Pie...............87

Pies
Kale and Squash Pie 51
Peachy Rhubarb Pie 118
PEI Potato Pie 71
Pumpkin Pie for Dr. Jim.......85
Spinach and Sausage Pie 89
S.berry Cream Cheese Pie...122
Strawberry Pie 121
Savoury Cauliflower Pie.......41
Summertime Veggie Pie 124
Tomato Bacon Pie.............98
Tomato Cheese Pie 98
Potato Stuffings
Baked Potato Stuffing........143
Basic Potato Stuffing.........147
Beef Stuffing 143
Broccoli Stuffing 143
Hot Milk Stuffing 144
Soufflé Potato Stuffing 147
Tasty Stuffing 144
Potatoes
Bacon/Chive Potato Patties ..78
Cheesy Potatoes...............76
Cottage Potatoes...............76
Crunchy Curried Salad........77
Eleanor's Mom's P.Salad 75
French Scalloped Potatoes ...71
Island Potato Bannock.........79
Margo's Swedish Potatoes 70
PEI Potato Pie 71
Potato Carrot Kugel............70
Slow Cooked Potatoes........72
Sweet and Sour Potatoes 78
Tasty Potato Slices............69
Twice Baked New Potatoes...77
Two Colour Baked Potatoes ..79
Pumpkin
Honey Pumpkin Pie 87
Lorraine's Walnut Cake 84
Pumpkin Bread 85
Pumpkin Cake Roll 86
Pumpkin Pie for Dr. Jim.......85
Radish
Radish and Squash Sauté......88
Radish Cucumber Side Salad .87
Radish Dill Slaw 88
Raspberries
Raspberry Cheesecake 117
Raspberry Orange Swirls.....116

Rhubarb
Rhubarb Cereal Crisp 118
Rhubarb PeachPie...............118
Rhubarb Pinwheels..............119
Rhubarb Muffins 119

Salad
Alice's Lime Cuke Salad 46
Broccoli Slaw Salad 24
Cataloupe Special 31
Crunchy Curried Potato Salad....77
Eleanor's Mom's Potato Salad ...75
Honey Dressed Spinach Salad 94
Honey Mustard Slaw 28
Okra, Wax Bean Salad............57
Radish Cucumber Side Salad 87
Radish Dill Slaw 88
Spinach Pasta Salad 90
Strawberry Salmon Salad 123
Summer Coleslaw 30
Summer Green Bean Salad.......15
Sweet Potato Salad...............82
Three Colour Bean Salad 12
Three Green Salad 54
Waldorf Salad.....................42

Salad Dressings
Asparagus Orange Mayonnaise..137
Barbeque Salad Dressing 133
Caesaar Salad Dressing.........137
Poppy seed Dressing 136
Flax Oil Salad Dressing 133
Golden Green Bean Dressing ...135
Green Salad Dressing...........135
Italian Salad Dressing 134
Maple Salad Dressing 134
Salad Greens Dressing..........137
Simple, Simple Salad Dressing ..136
Spicy Citrus Dressing 134
Spinach Salad Soy Dressing 135
Versatile Salad Dressing........133
Vinaigrette 136

Soup
Corn Chowder 43
Cream of Carrot Soup 33
Cream of Celery Soup 42
Grambie's Vegetable Soup.......99
Missouri Soup 40
Salmon Corn Chowder...........44

Spinach
Honey Dressed Spinach Salad 94
Spinach/Feta Cheese Quiche .89
Spinach and Sausage Pie 89

Spinach
Spinach Pasta Salad............90
Spinach Stuffed Tomatoes....93

Squash
Butternut Apple Crisp 94
Squash Casserole 95

Strawberries
Cheesecake Dip S.berries....123
Double Dipped Strawberries 120
Easy Strawberry Pie 122
S.berry Cream Cheese Pie...122
Strawberry Coffee Cake 120
Strawberry Pie 121
Strawberry Salmon Salad 123
Very Berry Choc. Shortcake.121

Sweet Potatoes
Cranberry S. Potato Muffins ..81
S.Potato Banana Muffins 81
Sweet Potato Layer Cake 80
Sweet Potato Quick Bread ...82
Sweet Potato Salad 82
Sweet Potato Scones 83
Tasty Glazed Sweet Potatoes 83
Upside Down S.Potato Cake ..84

Swiss Chard
Swiss Chard Sauté 95

Tomatoes
Tomato Bacon Pie.............98
Tomato Basil Squares..........96
Tomato Bread Casserole 97
Tomato Broccoli Cups 97
Tomato Cheese Pie 98
Tomato Salad Cups............99
Tomato Scallop 96

Turnip
Grambie's Vegetable Soup....99
Mash Turnips Extraordinaire 100
Turnip and Apple Bake.......100
Turnip Casserole 101

Watermelon
Melon Blueberry Treat 102
Show-off Melon Treat 32

Zucchini
Salmon Zucchini Cakes.......104
Stuffed Zucchini Boats.......107
Zucchini Carrot Cake..........105
Zucchini Carrot Muffins 102
Zucchini Chocolate Cake 104
Zucchini Choc. Chip Muffins 106
Zucchini Dipsticks 106
Zucchini Meatball Stew 103

PHOTO INDEX

Asparagus
Asparagus Rolls 38
Asparagus Tart ....cover
Layered Asparagus 19
Baking Beans
Saturday Night Baked Beans 55
Beets
Beet Relish.......................74
Beets Russian 92
Blackberries
Cinnamon Chocolate Fruit Tart ..20
Blueberries
Blueberry Oat Treats 74
French Toast Bake............145
Lemon Blueberry Scones 56
Bonus Recipe
Watermelon Slice Cookies 110
Broccoli
Broccoli and Cauliflower Bake ...92
Broccoli and Corn Bake 128
Cheesy Broccoli Pie 145
Scrumptous Broccoli Salad 19
Brussels Sprouts
Brown Sugar Glazed Sprouts 127
Cabbage
Surprise Coleslaw.................74
Cantaloupe
Cantaloupe Fruit Toss 19
Show-off Melon Treat 110
Carrot Glazes
Apple Glazed Carrots.............37
Carrots
Carrot and Pineapple Muffins 91
Carrot Chocolate Chip Loaf 56
Cream of Carrot Soup 55
Hidden Surprise Carrot Cake 92
Corn
Corn Chowder 55
Spicy Corn Spread 37
Cucumber
Alice's Lime Cucumber Salad 74
Cucumber Canapes...............38
Mustard Pickles..................128
Dips
Carrot Dip........................38
Curry Dip.........................38
Eleanor's Vegetable Dip..........38
Drinks
Fruit Smoothie 145
Honeydew Lemonade 91
Strawberry Lemonade...........91

Eggplant
Eggplant Bake 128
Kiwi
White Choc.Fruit Tart .....cover
Lettuce
Three Green Saland........cover
Onion
Onion and Cheese Tarts 145
Parsnips
Sweet Roasted Parsnips......127
Peas
Meatless Meatloaf 128
Peppers
Three pepper Veggie Toss...127
Potato Stuffings
Hot Milk Potato Stuffing 73
Potatoes
Bacon/Chive Potato Patties ..37
Cottage Potatoes...............92
Eleanor's Mom's P. Salad 74
Island Potato Bannock.........55
PEI Potato Pie 73
Potato Carrot Kugel............73
Sweet and Sour Potatoes 127
Tasty Potato Slices.............73
Two Colour Baked Potatoes ..73
Pumpkin
Pumpkin Bread 56
Radish
Radish Cuke Side Salad ....cover
Raspberries
Raspberry Orange Swirls 37
Salad Dressing
Delicious P.Seed Dressing..cover
Strawberries
Cheesecake Dip S.berries....109
Double Dipped S.berries.....109
Strawberry Pie 109
Very Berry Choc. Shortcake .109
Sweet Potatoes
Cranberry S.Potato Muffins...91
S.Potato Banana Muffins 91
Sweet Potato Layer Cake 20
Sweet Potato Quick Bread 56
Sweet Potato Scones 19
Upside Down S.Potato Cake ..20
Tomatoes
Tomato Basil Squares..........38
Tomato Cheese Pie 19
Tomato Salad Cups.............38
Turnip
Turnip and Apple Bake 92
Zucchini
Zucchini Choc. Chip Muffins ..91
Zucchini Meatball Stew 55

Paderno Pots Order Form

Paderno Pots are frequently referred to as "Pots for Eternity". You'll soon see why when you own one or more of these world class professional pots. Proudly used as the exclusive cookware for this publication, we're pleased to offer you a complete selection at Factory Direct pricing. See next page for detailed Paderno information.

Call us toll free at 1-800-363-7333, shop online at www.veseys.com or mail the form below to:

Canada:

Veseys Seeds Ltd.
PO Box 9000
Charlottetown, PE C1A 8K6

United States:

Veseys Seeds Ltd.
PO Box 9000
Calais, Me 04619-6102

PRODUCT DESCRIPTION	List $	Our Price save 40%	
_____ #82048 - 1.5L Saucepan w/cover	$109.	$ 64.95	_____
_____ #82049 - 2L Saucepan w/cover	$120.	$ 71.95	_____
_____ #82050 - 3L Saucepan w/cover	$146.	$ 87.95	_____
_____ #82051 - 4L Saucepan w/cover	$156.	$ 92.95	_____
_____ #82052 - 5L Dutch Oven w/cover	$179.	$106.95	_____
_____ #82053 - 6.5L Dutch Oven w/cover	$201.	$119.95	_____
_____ #82054 - 20cm Fry Pan	$ 99.	$ 59.95	_____
_____ #82055 - 24cm Fry Pan	$116.	$ 69.95	_____
_____ #82056 - 28cm Fry Pan	$146.	$ 87.95	_____
_____ #82057 - Double Boiler	$121.	$ 72.95	_____

Shipping and Handling $5. per pot	$ _____
subtotal	$ _____
Canadian residents add GST(7%) or HST(15%) NS,NB,NL	$ _____
Prince Edward Island residents only, add 10% PST	$ _____
Order TOTAL	$ _____

☐ Cheque enclosed or charge my   ☐ Visa   ☐ MC

Card # _____ Expiry _____

Signature _____

Name _____

Address _____

City _____ Prov/State _____ Code _____

Daytime Phone _____

Email _____

Paderno Pots

Paderno started in Prince Edward Island, Canada in 1979 with a vision of making cookware so good it would outlast anything in the kitchen. Since those early beginnings, their Pots for Eternity have become famous across Canada and into the United States. Not only has their vision of excellent performance and outstanding durability been the guiding light in making them Canada's only cookware manufacturer, it has helped them develop an ever widening range of kitchen products that continue to meet that standard. That's why Paderno Pots are guaranteed for 25 years.

Features and Design

Exceptional heat control

The aluminum bottom pad that is bonded to each stainless steel cooking vessel, transfers heat into the pot quickly and evenly, while the steel retains that heat inside the pot. Food cooks quickly and evenly, all the while using lower heat settings. An added bonus, the high quality pan bottom stays flat even after years of use.

Handles to hold on to

Paderno's handles are made from stainless steel, not plastic or wood, so they do not crack or chip. And because they are welded in place, not bolted, they stay on. Finally, the handles stay cool during use, because they are made from steel (a poor conductor of heat and the same reason these pots keep heat inside them so well).

Sleek styling, versatile use

The clean, sophisticated appearance of Paderno cookware makes it equally useful on the cooktop, in the oven or on the dining table. But these great looks make it easy to forget that this cookware is incredibly durable (thus the nickname 'Pots for Eternity'), dishwasher safe and comes with extensive warranty protection.

Lids and lips mean no drips

The special curved lip makes it easy to pour liquid from the cookware - without it ending up all over you or the floor! And covers are designed to provide a vapour-lock seal so all the goodness you are preparing inside the pot stays in the pot. All in all, using this cookware means less mess, less hassle...more satisfaction

Cookbook Order Form

Summer Savoury is a perfect gift for fellow gardeners, cooks and family. Let us help you with your gift giving by taking the hassle out of delivery.

On the next page, provide us the name and addresses of those to whom you wish to send our book and we'll gladly include a gift card with your order.

Call us toll free at 1-800-363-7333 or complete the forms below and mail your order to:

Canada:

Veseys Seeds Ltd.
PO Box 9000
Charlottetown, PE C1A 8K6

United States:

Veseys Seeds Ltd.
PO Box 9000
Calais, Me 04619-6102

_____# copies, item 819009 (Canada) @ $14.95 cdn funds _____
_____# copies, item 819019 (US)   @ $12.95 us funds _____
Shipping and Handling ($2.00 per book) _____
GST/HST 7% only (Canada only) _____

Order TOTAL $_____

Please complete Ship To information on next page

☐ Cheque enclosed or charge my   ☐ Visa ☐ MC

Card # _____ Expiry _____

Signature _____

Name _____

Address _____

City _____ Prov/State _____ Code _____

Daytime Phone _____

Email _____

161

Mail Order Form - Ship To:

Complete each block for every book you are sending.
Please photocopy if you require additional addresses:

Name _____

Address _____

City _____ Prov/State _____ Code _____

Gift card message: _____

_____

Name _____

Address _____

City _____ Prov/State _____ Code _____

Gift card message: _____

_____

Name _____

Address _____

City _____ Prov/State _____ Code _____

Gift card message: _____

_____

Name _____

Address _____

City _____ Prov/State _____ Code _____

Gift card message: _____

_____

Having first met in 1979 when teaching at the same elementary school, Eleanor and Faye quickly became close friends. Since that time they have continued to share their lifelong interests in baking, crafts, music and gardening.

Their professional teaching careers (classroom and music respectively), have contributed greatly to the organization and depth displayed in this authoritative collection of vegetable and berry recipes.

Eleanor and Faye both attribute their love of the kitchen to their mothers who enjoyed nothing more than having a large group of family for Sunday dinner.

Continuing this same tradition, they thoroughly love to bake for family and friends. Their local reputation as 'truly great cooks' now becomes international with the publication of *Summer Savoury*.

Eleanor MacDonald & Faye Barrett

"This is the kind of cookbook I love best because every page shows so much care and attention. Hats off to Faye and Eleanor for creating and presenting everything in such a mouth-watering way."
Aldona Satterthwaite, Editor, Canadian Gardening

"Feels like a down home Prince Edward Island picnic... easy, time-saving recipes." *Harrowsmith Country Life Magazine*

"Does anything taste as good as veggies picked in your own backyard? Summer Savoury features over 250 recipes and will inspire gardening chefs to create some mouthwatering dishes using homegrown vegetables and fruits."
Gardenwise Magazine

"Summer Savoury has a unique flair for all things retro - fun, old fashioned recipe ideas that harken back to family suppers and bake sales... it's full of favourites that inspire everyone to bring back the kitchen garden and turn the fruits (and vegetables) of their labour into classic home-style meals."
Catherine Therrien, Assistant Editor Gardening Life

SUMMER SAVOURY

ISBN 0-9738907-0-3

Can	$14.95
US	$12.95
Eur	€12.95
UK	£ 9.95

8 83112 11001 6

9 780973 890709